GROUP GUIDE

42 turnkey, easy-to-lead Bible study group sessions for men.

UNITED
FOR VICTORY

written by Lance Ingram and edited by Adam Tyson

United for Victory Group Guide

First edition, first print published by Warrior United, a part of Ingram Image. Visit us online at warriorunited.com.

Copyright © 2021 Lance Ingram. All rights reserved.

Content creation and creative direction by Lance Ingram.

Content and theological editing by Adam Tyson.

Grammatical editing by Kristie Garner and Drew Wright.

Cover design by Warrior United.

ISBN: 978-1-63752-519-7

FIGHT

Get a group of guys. Get equipped for victory.

"BE INSPIRED AS 42 MEN SHARE ABOUT BEING WARRIORS FOR JESUS."
- CHRIS TOMLIN

Tua Tagovailoa, Dave Ramsey, Craig Groeschel, and more.

**UNITED
FOR VICTORY**

assembled, directed, & edited by Lance Ingram

GET THE BOOK THAT GOES ALONGSIDE THIS STUDY AT WARRIORUNITED.COM

"And they have defeated [the accuser] by the blood of the Lamb and by their testimony." - Revelation 12:11

About the Contributors

Lance Ingram - Author

Lance Ingram is founder and owner of Warrior United, an organization in Birmingham, Alabama, that exists to equip men for spiritual victory through an encounter with Jesus. Their ultimate goal is to facilitate a culture where men get into groups, engage in authentic conversation, and encounter the presence of God.

Lance served as a core musician at one of the largest churches in the country, Church of the Highlands, leading tens of thousands into the presence of God behind Pastor Chris Hodges and Highlands Worship from 2009 to 2018. These supernatural encounters behind the drum kit inspired Lance's dynamic passion for men to know Jesus and obey Jesus so they can experience true peace and purpose in every area of their lives. This led Lance to author his book, *Warrior: Equipping Men for Spiritual Victory*, which has reached thousands of men with the Gospel across the country. Lance also assembled, directed, and edited *United for Victory*, the counterpart collective devotional of this study.

Many may recognize Lance as radio personality "Dr. Lou" from the nationally syndicated *Rick & Bubba Show*, which reaches more than a million listeners daily. He has been featured on *Sports Illustrated's si.com* for his clever college football satire on the wildly popular comedy program based in Birmingham, Alabama.

Lance is a successful entrepreneur, operating his marketing and web technologies small business since 2008. He is a communications graduate from Auburn University.

Lance and his wife, Brooke, have two sons, Crew and Oakland, and one daughter, Natalee.

Adam Tyson - Editor

Adam Tyson serves as Lead Pastor of Placerita Bible Church in Santa Clarita, California. Born and raised in a Christian home in Georgia, Adam attended medical school and became a physician's assistant, working in cardiovascular and thoracic surgery in Savannah for four years. While serving in his local church, he felt an overwhelming desire to pursue the glory of God through theological training and to serve the Lord in full-time ministry. Adam attended The Master's Seminary for both an M.Div. (2005) and D.Min. (2013). Shortly after in 2013, he began pastoring the people of Placerita Bible Church.

Many may recognize Adam from the pastoral role he has played in discipling rapper and fashion mogul Kanye West. Adam has traveled around the country sharing the Gospel at Kanye's Sunday Service events.

Adam has a passion for expository preaching, biblical counseling, worldwide missions, and reaching the community of Santa Clarita with the Gospel.

Adam and his wife, Lisa, have five children—Anna, Nate, Micaiah, Hudson, and Zoe.

Essentials for Leaders

About This Resource

This is a Bible study for men serious about fighting to become warriors for Jesus. Although it is a supplemental Bible study for the full-length collective book, *United for Victory*, this no-nonsense, gut-checking, Jesus-centered group guide can be used as a standalone study for men desiring discipleship. The 42 turnkey, easy-to-lead sessions outline the 42 topics covered in the full-length book and provide additional content for each subject, including over 340 Biblical principles, encouraging scriptures, and challenging questions to serve as a catalyst for conversation among men ages 13 and up in a group environment. Get a group of men and get ready for spiritual victory.

Easy to Lead

In designing this resource, our goal was not to create an exhaustive, overwhelming Bible study that intimidates a prospective leader with preparation requirements. Rather, we wanted to craft a simple resource that could quickly and effectively be referenced to generate Bible-centered conversation with practical application. Since many men juggle fast-paced schedules and have little extra time to prepare, our team aimed to tailor a condensed tool that would equip men as confident ministers of the Gospel without hassle.

Curriculum Format

Each session is consolidated into two pages and the curriculum begins on page 8. We highly recommend this curriculum be covered over the course of 42 sessions, as there is ample content from each of the 42 topics to fuel in-depth conversation for the duration of 30 minutes, one hour, or more if the men in your group are willing to participate. Although we strongly recommend the content be split into **42 sessions** (1 topic per session for 42 sessions), leaders may elect to adjust the format to **14 sessions** (3 topics per session for 14 sessions) or **6 sessions** (7 topics per session for 6 sessions) and simply abbreviate the amount of content from each topic that they cover. However, the more topics that are covered per session, the more challenging it will be to adequately discuss each topic.

No-Nonsense

This study was formatted with men in mind. Since men like to bypass the fluff and get to the point, the discussion format for each of the 42 topics is concise but thorough and follows the simple, patterned format below:

First, a straightforward Biblical principle.

Second, a supporting Bible passage. ***Reference 1:1***

Third, a short commentary and supplemental practical question.

It's easy: Principle, passage, commentary/question, repeat. If you can read, you can lead.

Note: if there are multiple questions included under a principle, ask the *first* question, let participants answer, and *then* ask the follow-up question(s). If any of the questions do not generate discussion among members, it is okay to leave them as rhetorical.

Guides for All

We recommend every group member acquire one of these group guides, as it allows them to get familiar with the content prior to each session by glancing over both the scriptures and questions in advance. Aside from its usefulness in the group context, this guide is also a valuable resource chock-full of Bible verses particularly relevant to a man's life.

The Goal of a Group

An effective group is one that simply combines the four following elements: **Truth, togetherness, talk, and transparency.** We know that where two or more are gathered around the Word, God *will* show up, and His Holy Spirit *will* change them (Matthew 18:20). We also know from experience that when men begin to share their victories and hidden struggles with one another, growth and healing are certain (James 5:16). The ultimate goal of a group experience is to let the combination of God's Word and thought-provoking questions establish spiritual and relational depth through authentic conversation. It's all about cultivating relationships. We also *strongly* recommend adding worship music as a background palette in your group environment to set the spiritual tone when possible. Worship music changes the atmosphere, softens our hearts, opens our eyes, and quietly encourages us to reflect. If anyone needs great worship music to supplement this group experience, check out our ever-evolving Warrior playlists at warriorunited.com.

Session Opener

Because this Bible study format goes in tandem with the full-length collective book, *United for Victory*, we suggest "breaking the ice" and establishing some initial dialogue at the beginning of each session by asking the following question: "Did you take away anything from this week's devotional story on [insert topic here]?" Another suggestion would be: "Does anyone have a specific scripture from this week's topic that challenged or encouraged them?"

Encourage Engagement

To increase engagement and promote interaction in your group, ask one of the members to read each of the verses out loud when the time comes to go over each passage in a session. This is a simple way to generate a more conversive culture within your group.

Embrace Transparency

Deep relationships only come from deep conversations. Deep conversations require authentic spiritual content. The more transparent the leaders and members are throughout this study, the more effective the time will be. If we are not willing to be honest with someone, then we cannot expect much growth or depth. No, that doesn't mean we need to air all of our "dirty laundry" among men who we've just met, but we absolutely need to find someone who can be entrusted with even our most secretive issues. Let's not be ashamed to get real and raw and voice our struggles. No one is going to be caught off guard because we all have our own issues!

Respect Confidentiality

If we are going to be bold enough individually to embrace transparency, then we need to be mature enough collectively to respect confidentiality. In a group setting, if other men decide to share their most intimate struggles, let's be sure to keep those admissions confidential. What is *shared* within a group *stays* within a group.

Topics

Intro
WARRIORS

God made us to be spiritual warriors. The focus of this study is to discuss what the Word says about our God-given design as warriors for Jesus.

We are in a cutthroat spiritual war with an intelligent, invisible opponent.

...Be strong in the Lord and in His mighty power. Put on all of God's armor so that you will be able to stand firm against all strategies of the devil. For we are not fighting against flesh-and-blood enemies, but against evil rulers and authorities of the unseen world, against mighty powers in this dark world, and against evil spirits in the heavenly places. **Ephesians 6:10-12**

We must realize that a continuous spiritual war exists in the supernatural that we cannot see, and it dictates everything in the natural that we do see. This reality is called spiritual warfare, where the forces of good and evil are wrestling in an unseen realm to impact our thoughts, decisions, and circumstances in the physical world. Do we expend more energy fighting in the natural against the people around us (which is wasteful)? Or are we wise enough to redirect our efforts toward fighting against the "evil authorities" in the supernatural (which is useful)? Why is prayer a crucial tactic to "stand[ing] firm against all strategies of the devil?"

We were created in God's image, and God's image is one of a warrior.

The Lord is a warrior; Yahweh is His name! **Exodus 15:3**

A brutal spiritual war exists, but there is zero reason to fear because Genesis 1:27 reminds us we are made in God's image, which means we are victorious *warriors*. Do you base your identity more off of what you see in a mirror—what the *world* has said you are—or are you firmly planted in who God says you are?

Jesus is the supreme spiritual Warrior who fights for righteousness.

Then I saw heaven opened, and a white horse was standing there. Its rider was named Faithful and True, for He judges fairly and wages a righteous war. His eyes were like flames of fire, and on His head were many crowns. A name was written on Him that no one understood except Himself. He wore a robe dipped in blood, and His title was the Word of God. The armies of heaven, dressed in the finest of pure white linen, followed Him on white horses. **Revelation 19:11-14**

The picture painted here in Revelation of Jesus is one of strength, courage, valor, and pure masculinity. Do we picture our Savior as one of unmatched strength or has the world watered down our picture of Jesus to be soft and feminine?

With Jesus, we can crush the enemy.

The God of peace will soon crush Satan under your feet... **Romans 16:20**

We have a real spiritual enemy who hates us with a passion. His aim is to destroy our lives (John 10:10). But when Jesus lives in us, we possess Satan-squashing power—the same devastating power that will bring the final victory over the enemy when Jesus returns to earth as He promised. Sin and death no longer have power over us because Jesus *lives*. Do we believe we can *crush* the enemy because of Jesus in us?

We must be trained and equipped by God to experience spiritual victory.

Praise the Lord, who is my rock. He trains my hands for war and gives my fingers skill for battle. He is my loving ally and my fortress, my tower of safety, my rescuer. He is my shield, and I take refuge in Him. He makes the nations submit to me. **Psalm 144:1-2**

On our own, we are inadequate, lacking the necessary skills for spiritual battle. But with God as our Ally, we are equipped with every ability needed for spiritual victory. How do we allow God to train us as warriors for spiritual battle?

Winning spiritual war begins with winning the internal battle of our desires.

So I say, let the Holy Spirit guide your lives. Then you won't be doing what your sinful nature craves. The sinful nature wants to do evil, which is just the opposite of what the Spirit wants. And the Spirit gives us desires that are the opposite of what the sinful nature desires. These two forces are constantly fighting each other, so you are not free to carry out your good intentions. **Galatians 5:16-17**

From the beginning of mankind with Adam and Eve, there has been an internal war waging in us between *our flesh* and *God's Spirit*. It is our way versus God's way. This battle within ourselves is challenging and constant, and victory depends on letting the Holy Spirit direct every thought and step. In Genesis 3, Adam and Eve were enticed by the devil with a lie—the prospect of "be[ing] like God." They chose their inclinations over God's instructions, and they forfeited God's best as a result. We *must* fight against our flesh to see spiritual victory. Does true freedom come from being able to do whatever our flesh desires or from adhering to the Holy Spirit's desires?

Warriors are empowered by God to be bold and self-disciplined.

For God has not given us a spirit of fear and timidity, but of power, love, and self-discipline. So never be ashamed to tell others about our Lord...With the strength God gives you, be ready to suffer with me for the sake of the Good News. **1 Timothy 1:7-8**

God calls us to audacious discipline that can withstand suffering for the sake of the Gospel. Proverbs 28:1 says the godly are "as bold as lions." Are we tenacious and self-disciplined as righteous reflections of Jesus? Or are we timid and self-indulgent?

We as ordinary men become extraordinary warriors when we spend time with Jesus and are filled with the Holy Spirit.

Then Peter, filled with the Holy Spirit, said to them..."There is salvation in no one else [but Jesus]! God has given no other name under heaven by which we must be saved." The members of the council were amazed when they saw the boldness of Peter and John, for they could see that they were ordinary men with no special training in the Scriptures. They also recognized them as men who had been with Jesus. **Acts 4:8, 12-13**

Notice how it wasn't smarts or seminary that enabled these men to do amazing things. It was spending time with Jesus and being filled with the Holy Spirit. Are we in a habit of "being with Jesus," *seeing* Him every day so that we remain Spirit-filled, passionate, and extraordinary for the advancement of the Gospel?

God, You engineered us to be spiritual warriors, to daily fight against the enemy and our natural desires, and to daily fight for the purity, righteousness, and character of Jesus Christ. Empower us and embolden us to fight for what matters. In Jesus' name we pray this.

1
PURPOSE

God intentionally created us for His purpose. The focus of this session is to discuss what the Word says about God's purpose for us as men.

We were created by Jesus' power for Jesus' glory.

Christ is the visible image of the invisible God. He existed before anything was created and is supreme over all creation, for through Him God created everything in the heavenly realms and on earth. He made the things we can see and the things we can't see—such as thrones, kingdoms, rulers, and authorities in the unseen world. Everything was created through Him and for Him. **Colossians 1:15-16**

No creation is an accident. God made everything "through [Jesus]" to worship Jesus. To discover the path for our purpose, we must go *through Jesus.* What are a few of the many ways we can honor God with our existence?

God made us to have a relationship with Him, but because of our sin, that relationship was broken. It was God's plan all along to restore that relationship through His perfect Son, Jesus.

But God showed His great love for us by sending Christ to die for us while we were still sinners. And since we have been made right in God's sight by the blood of Christ, He will certainly save us from God's condemnation. For since our friendship with God was restored by the death of His Son while we were still His enemies, we will certainly be saved through the life of His Son. **Romans 5:8-10**

Romans 6:23 reminds us that "the wages of [our] sin is death, but the free gift of God is eternal life through Christ Jesus." Purpose is found by turning from our sin and turning to God's Son, and 2 Timothy 1:9 says, "that was God's plan from the beginning of time—to show us His grace through Christ Jesus." Who has a testimony of being made right with God through repenting of your sin and receiving Jesus as your Savior? How has that brought you peace with God and new purpose in your daily life?

A relationship with Jesus is the only way to eternal life with our Creator.

Jesus told [Thomas], "I am the way, the truth, and the life. No one can come to the Father except through Me." **John 14:6**

Our world may say there are multiple avenues to heaven, but God says there is one. How do we stand boldly but lovingly on this truth?

God's purpose for each of us is to believe in Jesus and proclaim His name.

If you openly declare that Jesus is Lord and believe in your heart that God raised Him from the dead, you will be saved. **Romans 10:9**

Receiving Jesus is easy to do but following Him costs us everything. In turn, we experience indescribable peace and purpose. How often do others hear us proclaim the truth of Jesus Christ?

We all fall short of God's standard. Faith in Jesus is the only reparation.

For no one can ever be made right with God by doing what the law commands. The law simply shows us how sinful we are. But now God has shown us a way to be made right with Him without keeping the requirements of the law, as was promised in the writings of Moses and the prophets long ago. We are made right with God by placing our faith in Jesus Christ. And this is true for everyone who believes, no matter who we are. **Romans 3:20-22**

The world mistakenly says that if we are just "good," everything will work out favorably for us. Why do so many people prefer to work for salvation rather than simply accept God's free fix for our broken human condition?

Works-based salvation is impossible. Salvation-based works are inevitable.

God saved you by His grace when you believed. And you can't take credit for this; it is a gift from God. Salvation is not a reward for the good things we have done, so none of us can boast about it. For we are God's masterpiece. He has created us anew in Christ Jesus, so we can do the good things He planned for us long ago. **Ephesians 2:8-10**

There is no amount of works we can do to save ourselves, but when we are saved by Jesus, our salvation is manifest through works. What "good things" do you believe God planned for you—His masterpiece—to do to bring people to Jesus? What gifts and talents did He dynamically tailor for you to showcase for Him?

God's purpose from the beginning was to redeem us through the sacrifice of His Son.

For you know that God paid a ransom to save you from the empty life you inherited from your ancestors. And it was not paid with mere gold or silver, which lose their value. It was the precious blood of Christ, the sinless, spotless Lamb of God. God chose Him as your ransom long before the world began, but now in these last days He has been revealed for your sake. **1 Peter 1:18-20**

We are worth so much to our loving God. He *planned* to pay the price of our shortcomings—to redeem us—long before we even existed so that we would not be relegated to an "empty life" without purpose. Do we see Jesus' blood as an invaluable currency, worth far more than earth's precious metals?

God allows and ordains pain for His purpose of helping people.

[Joseph said,] "You intended to harm me, but God intended it all for good. He brought me to this position so I could save the lives of many people." **Genesis 50:20**

In this passage as Joseph addressed his brothers who had mistreated him for so long, we are reminded that nothing bad or harmful happens in your life outside of God's sovereign will. As Job 37 reminds us, God even controls every element of the weather—rain, thunder, lightning, ice, snow, wind, heat. Nothing is beyond His rule. But He *will* allow difficulty to discipline us and to accomplish His purpose. What pain in your life did God intend to help others?

God, You are our Creator. You made us intentionally to know You and to spend eternity with You. This purpose is realized only through having a relationship with Your Son, Jesus, and using our lives to help others discover this life-changing truth. Guide us to live out Your purpose. In Jesus' name we pray this.

2
SURRENDER

Surrender is essential for spiritual victory. The focus of this session is to discuss what the Word says about surrendering our lives to God's purpose.

God loves us so much that He surrendered His one and only Son, Jesus.

For this is how God loved the world: He gave His one and only Son, so that everyone who believes in Him will not perish but have eternal life. **John 3:16**

Spending eternity with us was so important to God that He gave up His Son to make it possible. Would you give up your child for someone else's benefit? What does God's sacrifice tell us about His love for us?

Self-denial and death of our own desires accompany surrender to Jesus.

Then [Jesus] said to the crowd, "If any of you wants to be my follower, you must give up your own way, take up your cross daily, and follow Me." **Luke 9:23**

Our journey with Jesus is better than our journey without Him, but it requires giving up what we want. Do we truly believe that God not only saves us but also has a greater fulfillment for us when we lay aside our desires?

Submission brings victory. Surrender brings salvation.

[Jesus said,] "If you try to hang on to your life, you will lose it. But if you give up your life for My sake, you will save it." **Matthew 16:25**

Everything in God's Kingdom feels backwards to the world's programming. This is the great paradox of the Gospel. The last are first. The weak are strong. The poor are rich. What part of your life is still under the control of culture's backwards thinking, making it difficult to let go of?

Surrender means we are God's messengers poised and ready to go.

Then I heard the Lord asking, "Whom should I send as a messenger to this people? Who will go for us?"

[Isaiah] said, "Here I am. Send me." **Isaiah 6:8**

The prophet Isaiah knew the urgency of surrendering his will to God so that others might know God. Where do you feel like God is calling you to share Jesus?

A relationship with Jesus makes earthly things seem hollow.

Yes, everything else is worthless when compared with the infinite value of knowing Christ Jesus my Lord. For His sake I have discarded everything else, counting it all as garbage, so that I could gain Christ and become one with Him... **Philippians 3:8-9**

Putting Jesus side-by-side with anything else makes it look like "garbage." Have you ever *seen* Jesus as the incomprehensible, incomparable, once-in-forever Man He is?

Surrender to Jesus involves letting spiritual light into *every* area of life.

So we are lying if we say we have fellowship with God but go on living in spiritual darkness; we are not practicing the truth. **1 John 1:6**

If we truly know God then we will live in the light of His Word. What habits are still in spiritual darkness that need to be surrendered to God?

We are all searching for peace. Surrender to Jesus is where we find it.

[Jesus said,] "I have told you all this so that you may have peace in Me. Here on earth you will have many trials and sorrows. But take heart, because I have overcome the world." **John 16:33**

Romans 8:17 reminds us that we are God's children and heirs of His glory, but that walking with Jesus will also bring some suffering. Who can attest to the "peace" that is found in Jesus even in the midst of the "trials and sorrows?"

God allows suffering to manifest our weakness and magnify His strength.

[The apostle Paul said,] "So to keep me from becoming proud, I was given a thorn in my flesh, a messenger from Satan to torment me and keep me from becoming proud. Three different times I begged the Lord to take it away. Each time He said, "My grace is all you need. My power works best in weakness." So now I am glad to boast about my weaknesses, so that the power of Christ can work through me." **2 Corinthians 12:7-9**

Surrender can make us *feel* defeated, but James 4:7 tells us that the combination of humbly surrendering ourselves before God and confidently standing up to the devil leads to surefire *victory*. Why is it so difficult for us as men to surrender? Could it have to do with our desire to be the strongest and our obsession to be in control?

We surrender every burden to Jesus because His name is higher than them all.

Therefore, God elevated [Jesus] to the place of highest honor and gave Him the name above all other names, that at the name of Jesus every knee should bow, in heaven and on earth and under the earth, and every tongue declare that Jesus Christ is Lord, to the glory of God the Father. **Philippians 2:9-11**

Name a challenge you're facing right now that is inferior to the name of Jesus.

God leads us on a truth-paved, hope-filled path when we yield to Him.

O Lord, I give my life to You. Show me the right path, O Lord; point out the road for me to follow. Lead me by Your truth and teach me, for You are the God who saves me. All day long I put my hope in You. Remember, O Lord, Your compassion and unfailing love, which You have shown from long ages past. **Psalm 25:1, 4-6**

God is a good God and wants to bless us in our journeys. How often do we voice our submission to God's way and our desperation for God's guidance? Do we deliberately seek God's wisdom even when our feelings are suppressed?

God, more than anything, You desire our surrender. You don't need us to be strong; You need us to be weak. You don't want us to be in control; You want us to submit to Your control. Let us humbly and gladly let go of our way, knowing that Your way leads to peace and purpose. In Jesus' name we pray this.

3
WORSHIP

God made everything to worship Him. The focus of this session is to discuss what the Word says about our God-given design as worshipers.

God designed all of creation to magnify Him and display His greatness.

The heavens proclaim the glory of God. The skies display His craftsmanship. **Psalm 19:1**

What is the most breathtaking, awe-inspiring place you have seen on earth? What does its beauty proclaim about God's character?

God is beckoning our worship through the vastness and intricacies of creation.

For ever since the world was created, people have seen the earth and sky. Through everything God made, they can clearly see His invisible qualities—His eternal power and divine nature. So they have no excuse for not knowing God. **Romans 1:20**

General revelation points to special revelation. Nature gives us an obvious supernatural glimpse into God's "eternal power and divine nature." But really, any and every creative element, even those authored by a human, that inspires our senses—a sight, a sound, a smell, a taste, or even a texture—is an extension of God's creativity. Because human creativity derives from *God's* creativity, a burst of inspiration from anything can be redirected from human admiration and converted to God worship. *Everything* but sin can be used to worship God. Is there a thing or person who gives you a tiny glimpse of God's creative power?

Worshiping anything but Jesus produces worthlessness for the Gospel.

[The Israelites] rejected [God's] decrees and the covenant He had made with their ancestors, and they despised all His warnings. They worshiped worthless idols, so they became worthless themselves... **2 Kings 17:15**

Worship will suffocate our sinful desires, or our sinful desires will suffocate our worship. Idols come when we try to make spiritual experiences out of secular elements. The fact that the *first* of the ten commandments in Exodus 20:3 says, "You must not have any other god but me," is proof that God values our worship more than anything else. Are there any "worthless" things that have stolen passion that belongs to Jesus?

Worship is stewarding our bodies as sacred, holy homes for God's presence.

Don't you realize that your body is the temple of the Holy Spirit, who lives in you and was given to you by God? You do not belong to yourself, for God bought you with a high price. So you must honor God with your body. **1 Corinthians 6:19-20**

We each are entrusted with a body to be the dwelling place of the Holy Spirit. We are to daily prepare it as a pure and clean mode of transportation as if we were driving around a VIP...because we are! Are we honoring God with what we consume and how we care for our bodies physically, emotionally, mentally, and spiritually?

Worship is a lifestyle that prioritizes purity of the eyes, ears, mouth, mind, heart, and body.

And so, dear brothers and sisters, I plead with you to give your bodies to God because of all He has done for you. Let them be a living and holy sacrifice—the kind He will find acceptable. This is truly the way to worship Him. **Romans 12:1**

Psalm 22:3 says God is holy. He is perfectly pure, set apart from everything and everyone. How do we keep our hearts, minds, and bodies worshipful to Him?

Worship is a grateful submission to God's will over our own.

[Jesus said,] "Father, if You are willing, please take this cup of suffering away from Me. Yet I want Your will to be done, not Mine." **Luke 22:42**

Jesus modeled for us that worship means yielding even when we do not understand. Is there a challenging situation in your life right now where you are yielding to God even though you don't understand?

God is a jealous God and wants our whole hearts.

[God said,] "When will you stop panting after other gods? But you say, 'Save your breath. I'm in love with these foreign gods, and I can't stop loving them now!'" **Jeremiah 2:25**

Everything the world offers is counterfeit. Nonetheless, what gods (little "g") do we see our culture "panting" for as sources of fulfillment? Truthfully, are we in love with these other gods or are we in love with Jesus?

Worshiping God with music is a front-line, winning weapon of spiritual war.

After consulting the people, [King Jehoshaphat] appointed singers to walk ahead of the [Judean] army, singing to the Lord and praising Him for His holy splendor. This is what they sang: "Give thanks to the Lord; His faithful love endures forever!" At the very moment they began to sing and give praise, the Lord caused [their enemies] to start fighting among themselves. **2 Chronicles 20:21-22**

Our passion for Jesus is directly tied to our worship of Jesus. When we lack zeal for Jesus, we likely are starving for an encounter with Him. Worship inspires and refreshes perspective. We win wars with worship. When we sing praise to God *before* our battles, He fights and wins them for us. Do you have a worship routine that cultivates God's presence in your homes, cars, and workplaces? What Christ-honoring music is most effective for you?

We worship God because of who He is and all He has provided for us.

Since we are receiving a Kingdom that is unshakable, let us be thankful and please God by worshiping Him with holy fear and awe. **Hebrews 12:28**

God's loving nature is evident in all He has given us—Jesus and eternal life—but what is an aspect of God's *character* that makes you want to worship Him?

God, You alone are worthy of our worship, and You made us to worship You alone. We lay aside every idol that has taken passion, focus, time, and energy that belongs to You, and we ask that You would cleanse our bodies to be pure and holy carriers of Your Spirit. In Jesus' name we pray this.

4
GOD'S WORD

God's Word is a warrior's source of spiritual survival and success. The focus of this session is to discuss how important God's Word is to being warriors for Jesus.

The Bible was written by humans, but every word was authored by God.

All Scripture is inspired by God and is useful to teach us what is true and to make us realize what is wrong in our lives. It corrects us when we are wrong and teaches us to do what is right. God uses it to prepare and equip His people to do every good work. **2 Timothy 3:16-17**

The Bible is God's Word. John 1:1 tells us that the Word has existed from the beginning and it *is* God. The Bible is the most powerful and versatile tool ever to exist, revealing God's nature and serving countless purposes. If we are not hearing from God, it is because we are not reading His voice. What purpose of the Word is special to you?

God's Word is literally alive and is dynamically intuitive.

For the word of God is alive and powerful. It is sharper than the sharpest two-edged sword, cutting between soul and spirit, between joint and marrow. It exposes our innermost thoughts and desires. **Hebrews 4:12**

The Bible has the ability to diagnose our hearts and our circumstances each day, no matter how unique they may be. Have you ever opened the Word to read it and it seemed to read you instead?

God's Word is the perfect navigator.

Your word is a lamp to guide my feet and a light for my path. **Psalm 119:105**

What dark situation in your past has God's Word brought light to and flawlessly navigated you through? How does the Bible presently shine forth to show you how to honor God ahead?

True success comes from frequently studying God's manual for our lives.

Study this Book of Instruction continually. Meditate on it day and night so you will be sure to obey everything written in it. Only then will you prosper and succeed in all you do. **Joshua 1:8**

We study what we are most passionate about, becoming experts in those areas. Do we know God's Word like we know business, sports, stocks, hunting, or music? How can we live out the Word if we do not know the Word?

Faith in Jesus thrives on consuming God's Word.

So faith comes from hearing...the Good News about Christ. **Romans 10:17**

Faith increases when we hear God's Word. Do you ever speak scripture out loud to increase your confidence in God or someone else's confidence in God?

God's Word is truth. Knowing truth brings freedom.

Jesus said to the people who believed in Him, "You are truly My disciples if you remain faithful to My teachings. And you will know the truth, and the truth will set you free." **John 8:31-32**

The enemy's weapon of choice is *lies*. Lies can only be identified by knowing truth. What is one lie you battle often and the truth you voice to defeat it?

The power of God's Word is realized when we obey it.

But don't just listen to God's word. You must do what it says...For if you listen to the word and don't obey, it is like glancing at your face in a mirror. You see yourself, walk away, and forget what you look like. **James 1:22-24**

God doesn't just want us to hear His word. He wants us to *obey* it. Once we obey, we experience its power. As renowned author Rick Warren has said, "Obedience unlocks understanding." What is one scripture that is easy to quote but difficult to model?

Evolving human knowledge is misleading. God's unchanging Word is trustworthy.

Don't let anyone capture you with empty philosophies and high-sounding nonsense that come from human thinking and from the spiritual powers of this world, rather than from Christ. **Colossians 2:8**

As 2 Timothy 4:3 says, we tend to "look for teachers who will tell [us] whatever [our] itching ears want to hear." Culture's clever, changing theories on life, happiness, relationships, and the afterlife can be convincing. How can we guard against falling for false teachings?

Rest and reliability are rooted in the wisdom of God's Word.

...the Lord says: "Stop at the crossroads and look around. Ask for the old, godly way, and walk in it. Travel its path, and you will find rest for your souls..." **Jeremiah 6:16**

God's Word is inerrant and infallible from cover to cover, with the Old Testament foreshadowing the New Testament with perfect consistency as it reveals God's story (Hebrews 8-9). The term "ancient" is used by critics of God's Word as an insult to its reliability and relevance in ever-progressing culture. However, God tells us that *rest* is found in the "old" way. How do we rest in *old wisdom* and not be deceived by *new knowledge?*

God calls us to work hard to share His Word with others.

...Don't be afraid of suffering for the Lord. Work at telling others the Good News, and fully carry out the ministry God has given you. **2 Timothy 4:5**

Knowing the Bible is the first step to sharing it. In order to share God's Word, it has to be a part of us. Are we consuming the Bible daily, even if it is only a verse or two?

God, Your Word is the most crucial element for victory in spiritual battle. It is our source of strength and hope and a light for our path. Give us passion and discipline to absorb Your Word daily. In Jesus' name we pray this.

5
PRAYER

Prayer is the lifeline that supplies power to a warrior. The focus of this session is to discuss what the Word says about the necessity of prayer in a warrior's life.

Jesus received His power by connecting to His Father in prayer.

Once Jesus was in a certain place praying. As He finished, one of His disciples came to Him and said, "Lord, teach us to pray, just as John taught his disciples."

Jesus said, "This is how you should pray: Father, may Your name be kept holy. May Your Kingdom come soon. Give us each day the food we need, and forgive us our sins, as we forgive those who sin against us. And don't let us yield to temptation." **Luke 11:1-4**

Notice how Jesus' priority in this prayer model was not His needs, but God's desires. Like a fuse, prayer was the conduit that connected Jesus to His power source—God, the Father—so that *His* will could be done. How often do we prioritize our prayers to focus on what God wants, not what we need?

God intended prayer to create intimacy, not a spectacle.

But when you pray, go away by yourself, shut the door behind you, and pray to your Father in private. Then your Father, who sees everything, will reward you. **Matthew 6:6**

Prayer is not to attract attention or impress others, but to cultivate a relationship with our Father. Do we have a time and place in which we talk to God privately each day? Does our routine involve being still and listening to Jesus' voice as Psalm 46:10 and John 10:27 instruct us to do?

Prayer is a discipline of constant awareness and gratefulness.

Devote [yourself] to prayer with an alert mind and a thankful heart. **Colossians 4:2**

First Thessalonians 5:17 urges us, "Never stop praying." Warriors are constantly connecting to God in conversation even without saying anything out loud. In our spirit, we quietly pray *about* every situation beforehand, and we pray *in* every situation as it is unfolding. We are aware of this reality: Prayer is the conduit through which spiritual war is fought. Prayer influences the supernatural, and the supernatural manifests itself in the natural. So, continuous prayer is pivotal to seeing victory in the natural. How can we quietly but effectively be on guard at all times against both temptation and discontent? And what percentage of your prayers would you estimate are prayers of thankfulness for what you *already* have, not requests of things you don't?

God desires our conversation and our burdens.

Give all your worries and cares to God, for He cares about you. **1 Peter 5:7**

Prayer is just a genuine conversation with a loving Father who *wants* to carry the worrisome weight we often lug around on our own. God *wants* to care for us. Do you have an accurate perspective of our Heavenly Father as loving, or do you mistakenly view Him as a frustrated Father?

Indescribable peace accompanies thankful prayer.

Don't worry about anything; instead, pray about everything. Tell God what you need, and thank Him for all He has done. Then you will experience God's peace, which exceeds anything we can understand. His peace will guard your hearts and minds as you live in Christ Jesus. **Philippians 4:6-7**

Worry and prayer cannot coexist because prayer is the antidote for anxiety. Why is it often harder to pray than to worry?

God intended His Holy Spirit to inspire and empower our prayers.

Pray in the Spirit at all times and on every occasion... **Ephesians 6:18**

It is crucial for us to remain pure vessels to attract God's Spirit so that *He* leads our prayer life. What differentiates a me-led prayer from a Spirit-led prayer?

God wants our requests to be for *His* glory and asked in Jesus' name.

[Jesus said,] "You can ask for anything in My name, and I will do it, so that the Son can bring glory to the Father. Yes, ask Me for anything in My name, and I will do it!" **John 14:13-14**

We misinterpret this passage when we perceive God as the 24/7, on-call dispenser of our wish list items. God doesn't just give us whatever earthly things we want because we ask for them in Jesus' name. Rather, God supplies the needs we have that specifically help us advance His Kingdom and bring Him glory. Do we truly believe we can change things in the natural by praying requests that are *focused on God's agenda* and are *brought in Jesus' name?*

When our requests involve making Jesus famous, we can be confident that He not only hears them, but will make them happen.

And we are confident that [Jesus] hears us whenever we ask for anything that pleases Him. And since we know He hears us when we make our requests, we also know that He will give us what we ask for. **1 John 5:14-15**

Faith and confidence go hand in hand. Both are anchored in certainty in God's goodness and trustworthiness. What prevents us from having a confident faith that God will deliver on His promises? Do we believe Matthew 6:8 and that God "knows exactly what [we] need even before [we] ask Him"?

Jesus prays for us, defending us and petitioning God on our behalf.

But if anyone does sin, we have an advocate who pleads our case before the Father. He is Jesus Christ, the one who is truly righteous. **1 John 2:1**

Romans 8:34 says that Jesus is our greatest supporter and is sitting at the right hand of God interceding for us in prayer. What humbles you most about the King of the world being *your* High Priest and pleading His blood to cover your sins?

God, prayer is how we access the supernatural current of Your unmatched power. It is a privilege to be able to talk to You, to hear from You, and to experience countless benefits from conversation with You. Make us disciplined, thankful, constant pray-ers. In Jesus' name we pray this.

6
PURITY

Purity of heart, mind, and body attracts God's presence into our lives. The focus of this session is to discuss what the Word says about the power of purity in a warrior's life.

We must engage in battle—fight—to maintain our purity.

In the spring of the year, when kings normally go out to war, David sent Joab and the Israelite army to fight the Ammonites. They destroyed the Ammonite army and laid siege to the city of Rabbah. However, David stayed behind in Jerusalem. Late one afternoon, after his midday rest, David got out of bed and was walking on the roof of the palace. As he looked out over the city, he noticed a woman of unusual beauty taking a bath. **2 Samuel 11:1-2**

King David was a dynamic warrior and worshiper. He is described in 1 Samuel 13:14 as "a man after [God's] own heart." He had an extraordinary passion for God. Yet, the moment David took a break from fighting, he was targeted by an opportunistic spiritual enemy who exploited his weakness (also the weakness of many men)—lust for beautiful women. David committed adultery (and eventually, murder) because he "stayed behind" instead of going to battle. Even the mightiest spiritual giants can face-plant if they relax for one second in spiritual battle, especially amidst sexual warfare. What avenues does Satan use to insert sexual temptation into our lives?

Humility and transparency with God lead us to purity.

Search me, O God, and know my heart; test me and know my anxious thoughts. Point out anything in me that offends You, and lead me along the path of everlasting life. **Psalm 139:23-24**

Do we humbly ask God daily to perform a spiritual inventory of our hearts, minds, and bodies? Do we *act* on what He says or does His guidance fall on deaf ears?

Jesus is the only purity in us.

We are all infected and impure with sin. When we display our righteous deeds, they are nothing but filthy rags. **Isaiah 64:6**

Our most exceptional human efforts to live righteously are "filthy" in God's eyes. Isaiah 43:25 says that it is Jesus and Jesus alone that "blot[s] out our sins" and makes us clean. Do we ever see ourselves as better or more worthy than others simply because of our behavior? Our actions definitely matter in God's eyes, but are we careful to acknowledge our unworthiness apart from Jesus' intervention?

Warriors do whatever it takes to eliminate impurity from our lives.

So put to death the sinful, earthly things lurking within you. Have nothing to do with sexual immorality, impurity, lust, and evil desires. Don't be greedy, for a greedy person is an idolater, worshiping the things of this world. **Colossians 3:5**

The word *emptiness* usually has a negative connotation, but the more empty we are of worldly things, the more space Jesus has to occupy. Is there any sin taking up space in our hearts that needs to be confessed and replaced with God's righteousness?

The enemy entices us to impurity with pleasure, possessions, and power.

For the world offers only a craving for physical pleasure, a craving for everything we see, and pride in our achievements and possessions. These are not from the Father, but are from this world. **1 John 2:16**

Satan uses the same "triple option" strategy on men that he used to tempt Jesus in the desert. He runs a tried-and-true, old-school scheme and doesn't deviate from it because...it works! Almost every sin originates from our desire for more pleasure (Old Testament goddess, Asherah), possessions (Old Testament god, Mammon), or power (Old Testament god, Baal). Which of these three—feeling good, attaining things, or gaining position and popularity—are you most susceptible to?

One step of repentance toward God restores unity and purity.

Come close to God, and God will come close to you. Wash your hands, you sinners; purify your hearts, for your loyalty is divided between God and the world. **James 4:8**

God runs quickly to us with forgiveness, healing, and restoration if we initiate just *one* step toward Him and away from worldly impurities. What typically keeps us from turning away from sinful habits? Pride? Defeat? Shame? Addiction? Deception?

Complete peace demands working toward complete purity.

...Let us cleanse ourselves from everything that can defile our body or spirit. And let us work toward complete holiness because we fear God. **2 Corinthians 7:1**

Where purity is not the priority, peace cannot be present. Our hearts and homes must be places of purity if we want them to be places of peace. Fearing God is loving Him enough to let Him cleanse us of every unholy habit. By Jesus' power, we *can* overcome any impure habit, but it may require some discomfort for our flesh. Are we "working" to starve that one habit that we have justified as our "struggle"?

Protecting our purity begins with protecting our eyes.

Turn my eyes from worthless things, and give me life through Your word. **Psalm 119:37**

My heart rarely goes anywhere my eyes have not already gone. Matthew 5:28 confirms this, saying that if we even *look* at a woman lustfully, we have already committed adultery in our *hearts*. If I keep my eyes pure, my heart will remain pure. But disciplined, Spirit-led eye control begins with intentional planning. Have you ever struggled with pornography or sexual sin? Since purity is never accidental, how do we prepare for the moment when a sexually enticing visual enters our periphery?

Obeying God's Word is the answer to purity.

How can a young person stay pure? By obeying Your word. **Psalm 119:9**

First Thessalonians 4:3 says, "God's will is for you to be holy, so stay away from all sexual sin." Holiness is impossible, especially for hormone-charged youth, without God's Word. What verses can help us stay sexually pure as warriors?

God, I want to fight for purity because it is the pallet where Your Spirit resides. Holy Spirit, help us do whatever it takes to guard our eyes and bring every thought into captivity to make it obedient to You. In Jesus' name we pray this.

7

FRIENDS & ACCOUNTABILITY

God made us for relationships. The focus of this session is to discuss what the Word says about God's intent for us to be connected to other warriors for Jesus.

We thrive when we are connected to other warriors.

Two people are better off than one, for they can help each other succeed. If one person falls, the other can reach out and help. But someone who falls alone is in real trouble. **Ecclesiastes 4:9-10**

We need each other, men. Like a wolf that studies his prey and then brings his pack to kill the lone sheep, our spiritual enemy targets the isolated. He celebrates when he sees separation from our Christian brothers. What are some examples of how we are "better" when we are connected to other warriors fighting for Jesus?

We inevitably become like our closest friends.

...For "bad company corrupts good character." Think carefully about what is right, and stop sinning. **1 Corinthians 15:33-34**

It was once said that "If you lie down with dogs, you get up with fleas." Our attitudes, beliefs, behaviors, convictions, and perspectives in life are shaped and influenced by the people with whom we spend the most time. This is why choosing friends who make us more like Jesus, not friends who make us more comfortable, is critical to spiritual victory. Are our three closest friends warriors who challenge us and sharpen us with the Word, as Proverbs 27:17 says?

Our closest companions must be disciples of Jesus Christ.

Don't team up with those who are unbelievers. How can righteousness be a partner with wickedness? How can light live with darkness? **2 Corinthians 6:14**

There can be no harmony between Christ and the devil according to verse 15 of this passage. Even if our immediate family members are not believers, we can choose to surround ourselves with God-fearing people from our local church. Why is it vital for our core, inner circle of friends to be Jesus followers so that we can reach the lost?

Sin thrives when we are disconnected from other warriors.

People who conceal their sins will not prosper, but if they confess and turn from them, they will receive mercy. **Proverbs 28:13**

What we cover, God will uncover; what we uncover, God will cover. Our "issues" can cultivate spiritual depth with other brothers if we are transparent about them. However, Proverbs 18:1 (ESV) says, "Whoever isolates himself seeks his own desire." How does revealing our sin to other men of God encourage lasting repentance?

Spiritual victory is built on biblical wisdom from multiple perspectives.

So don't go to war without wise guidance; victory depends on having many advisers. **Proverbs 24:6**

Proverbs 15:22 tells us that "plans go wrong for lack of advice," precisely the reason why having a 30,000-foot view of your circumstances from several vantage points greatly enhances your chance of spiritual success. Who has a Christian spiritual mentor and how has his wisdom been instrumental in bringing you spiritual victory?

A real friend will kindly deliver biblical truth to us even if it hurts.

An open rebuke is better than hidden love! Wounds from a sincere friend are better than many kisses from an enemy. **Proverbs 27:5-6**

Proverbs 17:17 says, "A friend loves at all times," but a genuinely loving friend offers Scripture-backed correction and inconvenient accountability because it has the *best* interest of the recipient in mind. Has a Christian friend ever confronted you with a brutal truth while others in your life were endorsing your sinful behavior? Who cares about you more—someone who doesn't want to *hurt your feelings now* or someone who doesn't want to *see you suffer later?*

To hold others accountable, we must first hold *ourselves* accountable.

[Jesus said,] "And why worry about a speck in your friend's eye when you have a log in your own?...Hypocrite! First get rid of the log in your own eye; then you will see well enough to deal with the speck in your friend's eye." **Matthew 7:3,5**

We must always clean house first in our own hearts, whatever the sin may be. Once that happens, God will make us useful in helping others deal with their sin. Why is it effortless to criticize sins with which we don't struggle?

Accountability involves confrontation.

[Jesus said,] "If another believer sins, rebuke that person; then if there is repentance, forgive." **Luke 17:3**

Jesus instructs us to first be inward-focused on our own sin, not casting judgment on another's heart, but He makes it clear that calling out the sin of other believers is needed. We don't *condescendingly judge hearts*, but we *kindly confront habits* of Christian brothers. What does loving confrontation look like to you?

Gentleness and humility accompany biblical accountability.

Dear brothers and sisters, if another believer is overcome by some sin, you who are godly should gently and humbly help that person back onto the right path. And be careful not to fall into the same temptation yourself. Share each other's burdens, and in this way obey the law of Christ. **Galatians 6:1-2**

Accountability is crucial for survival in spiritual warfare because it carries, not ostracizes, a brother. We are called to assist, not abandon a warrior being exploited in battle. How can we practically "share each other's burdens" and "help [each other] back onto the right path?"

God, we need other men in our lives who are passionate about living for You. Let us realize how pivotal it is to remain connected to Christian warriors through every season and to welcome bold, honest accountability. Let us exemplify truth and extend grace to everyone, especially the lost. In Jesus' name we pray this.

8
INTEGRITY

Integrity is the foundation of a warrior. The focus of this session is to discuss what the Word says about God's desire for us to model wholeness and consistency as warriors for Jesus.

Jesus *is* integrity and consistency.

Jesus Christ is the same yesterday, today, and forever. **Hebrews 13:8**

There is one flawless example of wholeness. His name is Jesus. He is complete and He never changes. What are some ways we strengthen our families by shadowing the rock-solid reliability and consistency of Jesus?

Storing God's Word in our minds and hearts sustains integrity.

I have hidden Your word in my heart, that I might not sin against You. **Psalm 119:11**

Integrity is based on a standard defined by the wisdom of God's Word. It is impossible to live by a set of principles that we have not absorbed in our souls. How does accumulating God's Word in our hearts help us maintain wholesomeness?

Our hearts are corrupt by nature.

The human heart is the most deceitful of all things, and desperately wicked. Who really knows how bad it is? But I, the Lord, search all hearts and examine secret motives. I give all people their due rewards, according to what their actions deserve. **Jeremiah 17:9-10**

God's design of every human is flawless; every human's desires are at fault. We must learn to separate our pure design from our impure desires, recognizing that selfishness, deception, and secretiveness are not God's intent. Knowing this truth, how do we fight to neutralize the imperfect natural desires that contradict our Creator's perfect supernatural design?

Men of integrity *apply* Biblical knowledge and *model* what they profess.

Remember, it is sin to know what you ought to do and then not do it. **James 4:17**

Someone once said, "I no longer listen to what people say, I just watch what they do. Behavior never lies." The most impactful lesson we teach our wives, kids, friends, colleagues, and acquaintances is not what we say, but what we do. Is there any area in our lives where we are teaching one thing but displaying another?

Warriors do whatever is necessary to keep our eyes from impurity.

I will refuse to look at anything vile and vulgar... **Psalm 101:3**

Guarding our eyes is consequential in maintaining our integrity. Second Timothy 2:22 says, "*Run* from anything that stimulates youthful lusts..." This may be the only trustworthy tactic to guarding our eyes: rotate our necks away from the stimulant and flee the scene immediately! We must *move*. Are we adamant about protecting our eyes with self-discipline and the Word of God even if no one is watching us?

God knows and sees everything, and the supernatural consequences of His omniscience cannot be avoided.

Nothing in all creation is hidden from God. Everything is naked and exposed before His eyes, and He is the one to whom we are accountable. **Hebrews 4:13**

Integrity is about wholeness, but it is also about sameness. Warriors are the same men in public that we are in private. We must understand that God sees "everything we do, including every secret thing, whether good or bad," even if our wives or bosses don't see it (Ecclesiastes 12:14). And ultimately, the ramifications of divine accountability far outweigh any other. Do you think it is possible for us to manufacture authentic peace on our own while we are concealing sin? (See James 1:15 and the inevitable result of "death" that sin produces.)

Accumulating honesty is more valuable than accumulating money.

Better to be poor and honest than to be dishonest and rich. **Proverbs 28:6**

Money can consume our hearts and compromise our integrity. Are we completely honest in reporting every penny on our taxes? Logging our work hours? Paying subcontractors? Divulging contract details? Telling our wives about expenditures?

God desires complete—not partial—holiness.

Now may the God of peace make you holy in every way, and may your whole spirit and soul and body be kept blameless until our Lord Jesus Christ comes again. **1 Thessalonians 5:23**

When you insert $0.99 into a vending machine to purchase a candy bar that costs $1.00, you still don't receive that delicious candy bar. God's best comes when we give Him *all*—not most or *almost* all—of us. Are we aiming to "be perfect, even as [our] Father in heaven is perfect," as Jesus urged in Matthew 5:48? Or are we settling for just being "better than the next guy?"

Warriors model the integrity of Jesus to society.

We are careful to be honorable before the Lord, but we also want everyone else to see that we are honorable. **2 Corinthians 8:21**

Isaiah 61:3 describes an upright man as a "great oak [tree]" planted by God that reflects His glory. Do others see us as solid, immovable, and unbreakable because of the righteousness of Jesus that we carry in our core?

We develop integrity in our children by teaching them God's Word.

And you must commit yourselves wholeheartedly to [God's] commands...Repeat them again and again to your children. Talk about them when you are at home and when you are on the road, when you are going to bed and when you are getting up. Tie them to your hands and wear them on your forehead as reminders. Write them on the doorposts of your house and on your gates. **Deuteronomy 6:6-9**

Do our kids hear and see God's Word daily? Do we intertwine it with every situation?

God, make us men who are wholly pure, completely consistent, and perfectly dependable. Let Jesus—*the* model of integrity— fortify us with His righteousness. In Jesus' name we pray this.

9
HUMILITY

Humility is the defining characteristic of Jesus Christ. The focus of this session is to discuss what the Word says about considering God and others above ourselves.

Jesus *is* humility.

*You must have the same attitude that Christ Jesus had. Though He was God, He did not think of equality with God as something to cling to. Instead, He gave up His divine privileges; He took the humble position of a slave and was born as a human being. When He appeared in human form, He humbled Himself in obedience to God and died a criminal's death on a cross. **Philippians 2:5-8***

Having the attitude of Jesus means obedience to God and service of others. Jesus' ultimate humility was demonstrated by voluntarily dying. What specific examples in Jesus' life displayed perplexing humility as He submitted to God's will and served others? What things do we need to die to in order to be humble as well?

Humility is prioritizing service over status.

*[Jesus said,] "And since I, your Lord and Teacher, have washed your feet, you ought to wash each other's feet. I have given you an example to follow. Do as I have done to you." **John 13:14-15***

The King of the universe got down on His knees to scrub the nasty, crusty feet of a group of common, sinful men...the night before He was to be butchered. One of Jesus' final lessons exhibited this perplexing humility. Why is it easy to serve those with status but difficult to sacrifice for those with nothing to offer in return?

Repentance is the epitome of humility.

*[The Lord said,] "Then if My people who are called by My name will humble themselves and pray and seek My face and turn from their wicked ways, I will hear from heaven and will forgive their sins and restore their land." **2 Chronicles 7:14***

It is remarkably difficult for us as men to admit when we are wrong and change our direction to make it right, but that is what God defines as the precursor for forgiveness, healing, and restoration. What usually prevents us from confession and repentance? Is it pride? Fear? Shame? Guilt? Embarrassment?

Humility honors authority and authorizes us to be honored.

*...You who are younger must accept the authority of the elders. And all of you, dress yourselves in humility as you relate to one another, for "God opposes the proud but gives grace to the humble." So humble yourselves under the mighty power of God, and at the right time He will lift you up in honor. **1 Peter 5:5-6***

When we are humble enough to respect spiritual authority within the church, we honor *God's* authority. God responds in the supernatural by reciprocating that honor. God's Word is our ultimate standard, but the same honor for authority can be applied in the office, on the football field, and in our communities. Even in disagreement, we can show respect, as Shadrach, Meshach, and Abednego demonstrated with King

Nebuchadnezzar in Daniel 3. Who is the most difficult person to honor in your life, and how can you be more humble "as you relate to [him or her]?"

When we practice humility, God promotes us.

[Jesus said], "When you are invited to a wedding feast...take the lowest place at the foot of the table. Then when your host sees you, he will come and say, 'Friend, we have a better place for you!' Then you will be honored in front of all the other guests. For those who exalt themselves will be humbled, and those who humble themselves will be exalted." **Luke 14:8,10,11**

Proverbs 29:23 says, "Pride ends in humiliation, while humility brings honor." Humility is not a means to attain a spotlight, but Jesus promises that intentionally taking a lower position on earth inevitably elevates our position in heaven. What are some practical ways we can "take the lowest place" in our workplaces, churches, and homes?

If we want to be wise, we must first be humble.

Pride leads to disgrace, but with humility comes wisdom. **Proverbs 11:2**

Since Jesus is the Word, and Jesus is also humility, the Word could be considered humility. It would make sense, then, that pride constricts the Word from flowing through us. What area of pride could be obstructing the wisdom of God's Word from flowing through us?

Warriors exterminate prideful, self-admiring thoughts.

...I give each of you this warning: Don't think you are better than you really are. Be honest in your evaluation of yourselves, measuring yourselves by the faith God has given us. **Romans 12:3**

Paul's stinging reminder to us is that our *faith in Jesus* is the only impressive part of us. Do we have any God-given attributes, talents, or accomplishments that we mistakenly credit to ourselves? How do we shut down these entry points of pride?

Blessings follow *true* humility.

True humility and fear of the Lord lead to riches, honor, and long life. **Proverbs 22:4**

When Jesus defeated death and rose from the grave, He could have easily done so with a huge crowd watching, reporters on site and in awe. Instead, much like His birth, Jesus brought no fanfare or flash. He *humbly* conquered the most incredible feat in human history with no spectators in sight. This a far cry from our attention-obsessed, narcissistic culture that claims humility but exudes pride. False humility runs rampant among men motivated by promotion and position, but humility is not a show. How can we guard ourselves from the masquerade of manufactured humbleness that conceals silent arrogance?

God, just like Your Son demonstrated for us, we are nothing but Your servants. We humble ourselves, turn from our sin, and pour out our lives to wash Your feet and the feet of those You place in our paths. Let us honor the dishonorable, love the unlovable, and bless the disagreeable as we humbly put our interests aside. In Jesus' name we pray this.

10
PASSION

Passion for Jesus drives a warrior to obey God. The focus of this session is to discuss what the Word says about keeping our passion fixed on Jesus, not on the world.

Jesus' life and death are the embodiment of pure passion.

[Jesus] was despised and rejected—a man of sorrows, acquainted with deepest grief. We turned our backs on Him and looked the other way. He was despised, and we did not care. Yet it was our weaknesses He carried; it was our sorrows that weighed Him down...He was pierced for our rebellion, crushed for our sins. He was beaten so we could be whole. He was whipped so we could be healed. **Isaiah 53:3-5**

If you're wondering what passion looks like, just look at Jesus' life...*and* death. The very definition of passion is manifest in the obedient life and sacrificial death of Jesus. He surrendered every thought and action to the Father when He was on earth, even relinquishing His life, being *slaughtered* because of the intense love He had for God and us. What does Jesus' unwavering obedience teach us about passion? Is it just emotion? Or is it something far more steady and substantial?

God wants our passion, and giving Him our passion means we are *all* in.

Jesus replied, "The most important commandment is this: 'Listen, O Israel! The Lord our God is the one and only Lord. And you must love the Lord your God with all your heart, all your soul, all your mind, and all your strength.'" **Mark 12:29-30**

"Partial passion" is an oxymoron. Jesus tells us that God desires *all* our heart, *all* our soul, *all* our mind, and *all* our strength. Passion *involves* emotion, but it is not *just* emotion. It is an alignment of our entire being with God's purpose for our lives. This is a difficult question to pose, but are we more passionate about our favorite sports team or our Savior? Do we invest more of our time, money, energy, and emotion in hunting for deer, restoring cars, and playing guitars, or spreading the Gospel?

We are the only representation of Jesus that many will ever experience.

So we are Christ's ambassadors; God is making His appeal through us. We speak for Christ when we plead, "Come back to God!" **2 Corinthians 5:20**

Just like a brand ambassador for a company, we are to passionately illustrate the "brand" of Jesus Christ. We display His qualities and values. What characteristics of Jesus should magnetize others to us as we fervently model His life to the lost? Are our words and actions accurately and attractively depicting Jesus?

A passionate warrior strategizes to serve the Lord and spread the Gospel.

Never be lazy, but work hard and serve the Lord enthusiastically. **Romans 12:11**

Passion prompts strategy. If I asked the three closest people to you what your greatest worldly passion was for, what would they say? Would it be music? Business? Sports? Vehicles? Now consider this: How are you practically utilizing that specific passion to connect people with Jesus? How can we get more creative in using our work, hobbies, and interests more effectively to serve Jesus?

Warriors deliberately quench our thirst and find our hope in Jesus.

*As the deer longs for streams of water, so I long for you, O God. I thirst for God, the living God...Why am I discouraged? Why is my heart so sad? I will put my hope in God! I will praise Him again—my Savior and my God!...**Psalm 42:1-2,5-6***

Describe the most passionate person you know and what they are passionate about. Would you agree that if we are not careful, we can actually "thirst" for more of a *worldly* passion and even look to it for "hope" when we are "discouraged?"

We are either loving Jesus or loving the world; we cannot do both simultaneously.

*Do not love this world nor the things it offers you, for when you love the world, you do not have the love of the Father in you. **1 John 2:15***

James 1:8 says that sometimes "[our] loyalty is divided between God and the world" and that it makes us "unstable in everything [we] do." We can easily determine whether activities or affiliations have become idols by examining how much they control our time, money, efforts, emotions, attitudes, and principles. If you had to choose a worldly interest, hobby, or thing that competes most for the passion that Jesus desires and deserves, what would it be? What *idols* do we sometimes write off as "passions" that compromise our spiritual stability?

Passionate pursuit of God brings freedom and restoration.

*"If you look for me wholeheartedly, you will find Me. I will be found by you," says the Lord. "I will end your captivity and restore your fortunes..." **Jeremiah 29:13-14***

Israel needed to look to God to be set free from their captivity and restore their status. How do we practically "look for God wholeheartedly" on a daily basis? Is there anything you are asking God to restore right now?

Our passion for Jesus grows when we crucify our passion for sin.

*Those who belong to Christ Jesus have nailed the passions and desires of their sinful nature to His cross and crucified them there. Since we are living by the Spirit, let us follow the Spirit's leading in every part of our lives. **Galatians 5:24-25***

What we feed will grow; what we starve will die. If we want more passion for Jesus, we must follow the Holy Spirit's prompting to starve sinful desires and habits in "*every* part of our lives." However, taking the approach of "stop sinning" is never sustainable. As humans, we lack the power to simply *stop* for an extended period of time. We must instead *substitute* sin with the Holy Spirit. We don't just stop; we substitute! We first subtract sin and then substitute with the Spirit so the void is filled with substance. This may be a question you want to discuss with someone one-on-one after this session, but what sinful passion in your life needs to be "nailed to [Jesus'] cross" and replaced with the Spirit?

God, You desire all of our passion. We declare that encountering Your Son, Jesus, and helping others do the same, is our passionate purpose. Destroy our passion for sin and the world, and fuel our passion for Your Kingdom as we strategize to reach others with the Truth. In Jesus' name we pray this.

11
COMMITMENT

Commitment to God's way brings abundance. The focus of this session is to discuss what the Word says about committing our lives to the glory of Jesus.

Commitment to God brings success for us.

Commit your actions to the Lord, and your plans will succeed. **Proverbs 16:3**

In John 2:5, Jesus' mother reveals to us the key to seeing blessings and miracles— to "do whatever He tells you." They had run out of wine at a wedding celebration in Cana, and she knew that Jesus would bring abundance from emptiness *if* they would listen to His instruction first. What is God calling you to do right now for His Kingdom? Do you truly believe it will succeed if you "commit your actions to [Him]"?

Commitment produces joyful toughness.

We can rejoice, too, when we run into problems and trials, for we know that they help us develop endurance. And endurance develops strength of character, and character strengthens our confident hope of salvation. **Romans 5:3-4**

Like a boxer that fights through the ups and downs of all twelve rounds, we as warriors are resilient and durable because of Jesus in us and because of the prize at the end of the match. How can we maintain a joyful toughness even when circumstances are rough? And how can our *words* affect our attitude and endurance both positively and negatively?

Committed warriors embrace life's challenges as faith builders.

So be truly glad. There is wonderful joy ahead, even though you must endure many trials for a little while. These trials will show that your faith is genuine. It is being tested as fire tests and purifies gold—though your faith is far more precious than mere gold. **1 Peter 1:6-7**

What trial are you having trouble "[being] glad" about right now? What could God be burning away and purifying during this difficult time? What specific promises can you use to replace the discouraging thoughts in your head?

Commitment to our wives is evidenced by selfless sacrifice for them.

For husbands, this means love your wives, just as Christ loved the church. He gave up His life for her to make her holy and clean, washed by the cleansing of God's Word. **Ephesians 5:25-26**

The purest, most peace-filled version of our wives will manifest when *they* become the priority and our interests take a back seat. This can only happen as we become living reflections of God's Word. So, we literally *become* God's Word, and she is cleansed of all the anger, animosity, and insecurity as a result. This is a sacrificial love that involves a daily dying to ourselves. Would your wife say she is the number one priority in your life? If not, what would she say is first in your rankings? What are some ways we can consistently serve our wives? And what specific daily chores can we humbly knock out to ease our wives' stress?

A warrior husband is committed to gently leading and considering his wife.

In the same way, you husbands must give honor to your wives. Treat your wife with understanding as you live together. She may be weaker than you are, but she is your equal partner in God's gift of new life. Treat her as you should so your prayers will not be hindered. **1 Peter 3:7**

The prerequisite to *leading* a wife is *following* Jesus. Our commitment to Him results in our consideration of her. The more time we invest seeking to understand our wives, the more genuinely we can honor them. Are there any areas in which we are dominating and inconsiderate, failing to represent that gentle leadership of Jesus in our marriages?

Warriors are committed to sexual purity and Spirit-led eye-control.

I made a covenant with my eyes not to look with lust at a young woman. **Job 31:1**

Romans 8:6 reminds us that "letting [our] sinful nature control [our] mind leads to death. But letting the Spirit control [our] mind leads to life and peace." If we want purity and peace, we must be committed to letting the Holy Spirit control our *eyes*, because *seeing* something tempting always begins the almost unstoppable downhill momentum that culminates in sexual sin. What medium poses the greatest temptation for sexual immorality? Is it our phones? Magazines? Social media? A coworker? What Bible verses can help us with this battle?

Warriors just keep getting back up.

The godly may trip seven times, but they will get up again. But one disaster is enough to overthrow the wicked. **Proverbs 24:16**

Because of God's grace, we can *always* get back up and get back in the fight. Perseverance and persistence are essential for spiritual victory. What keeps you committed after the devastating blows that life and our disobedience often bring?

Warriors are committed to leading our families to Jesus.

...But as for me and my family, we will serve the Lord. **Joshua 24:15**

What are we doing and saying on a daily basis to truly lead our families to Jesus?

Our allegiance to family pales in comparison to our alliance with Jesus.

[Jesus said,] "If you want to be my disciple, you must, by comparison, hate everyone else—your father and mother, wife and children, brothers and sisters—yes, even your own life. Otherwise, you cannot be my disciple." **Luke 14:26**

This verse doesn't mean we should actually *hate* our families but that we must prioritize obedience to God's Word over even our family's earthly desires. Has your commitment to God's Word ever resulted in conflict with your immediate family or extended family? How can we humbly remain steadfast in obedience while lovingly disagreeing with those closest to us? Why is it key for us to love long before lecturing?

God, we are committed to You and Your Word. We resolutely commit to leading our wives, families, and the lost to Jesus. Make us loyal, joyful, tough, and wise as we walk through the challenges of life. In Jesus' name we pray this.

12
LOVE

Love is who God is and who God made us to be. The focus of this session is to discuss what the Word says about loving God and loving others.

God proved He *is* love by sending Jesus to die so that we could live.

Dear friends, let us continue to love one another, for love comes from God. Anyone who loves is a child of God and knows God. But anyone who does not love does not know God, for God is love. God showed how much He loved us by sending His one and only Son into the world so that we might have eternal life through Him. This is real love... ***1 John 4:7-10***

God's unrivaled act of love—giving up His Son for us—defines "real love." If you have a child, you likely understand the enormous, indescribable affection that a father has for his kids. What does it say about God's love for *us* that He gave up His *only* Son so we could one day spend eternity with Him?

God's love for us never stops, no matter what we have done.

For the Lord is good. His unfailing love continues forever, and His faithfulness continues to each generation. ***Psalm 100:5***

First John 3:1 says, "See how very much our Father loves us, for He calls us His children, and that is what we are!" We are God's children, and God's love for His children has no end or boundary, regardless of our past mistakes. Is there anything that needs to be released right now—regret, guilt, fear, or shame—that has kept you from receiving the boundless, forgiving love that God has for you?

God showed His extraordinary love by offering us His Holy Spirit.

...For we know how dearly God loves us, because He has given us the Holy Spirit to fill our hearts with His love. ***Romans 5:5***

God's love is so obvious. Not only did He give us His Son, but He then gave us His tangible presence here on earth—the Person of the Holy Spirit—to be with us 100% of the time. Talk about a gift! Do we ask for His Spirit to be in us every day?

If we love Jesus, we will love people by living the Truth and giving the Truth.

Jesus repeated the question: "Simon son of John, do you love Me?"

"Yes, Lord," Peter said, "You know I love You."

"Then take care of My sheep," Jesus said. ***John 21:16***

Loving Jesus translates to loving people. Loving people translates to serving people. Serving people translates to giving them the Gospel. What are we doing to help the lost sheep be found and the found sheep to help more lost sheep?

Love is not just words; it is actions.

Dear children, let's not merely say that we love each other; let us show the truth by our actions. **1 John 3:18**

Love is not a lighthearted feeling; it is a serious commitment. It isn't just words; it is actions. In 1 Corinthians 16:14, we are urged to "*do* everything with love." Is there any part of our lives where we speak love but fail to demonstrate it?

Nothing we possess or accomplish matters if we do not love others.

If I had the gift of prophecy, and if I understood all of God's secret plans and possessed all knowledge, and if I had such faith that I could move mountains, but didn't love others, I would be nothing. **1 Corinthians 13:2**

We are a contradiction to God's nature if love does not accompany every word we say, every thought we think, and every action we take. That is why we are of zero value in building God's Kingdom without expressing love. Love is more important than every other spiritual gift. What pollutes our hearts from exhibiting the love of Jesus? Jealousy? Anger? Bitterness? Comparison? Unforgiveness? Judgment? Pride?

Love means praying blessings over those that hurt, annoy, or anger you.

Bless those who persecute you. Don't curse them; pray that God will bless them. **Romans 12:14**

People mess up. And people will be people, wherever they are...even within the church. That is why Ephesians 4:2 says, "Always be humble and gentle. Be patient with each other, making allowance for each other's faults because of your love." We make room for people's mistakes before they even happen. Pastor Chris Hodges, Lead Pastor of Church of the Highlands, says this about resilient love: "The world is full of hard hearts and thin skin. We need to have the opposite—soft hearts and thick skin." The most mature warrior isn't easily offended, and he *prays favor* over those that offend him—that God would grant the offender forgiveness. Why is it so difficult to "bless" those that hurt us?

Warriors keep on loving and let *God* handle retaliation.

Dear friends, never take revenge. Leave that to the righteous anger of God. For the Scriptures say, "I will take revenge; I will pay them back," says the Lord. Instead, "If your enemies are hungry, feed them. If they are thirsty, give them something to drink. In doing this, you will heap burning coals of shame on their heads." Don't let evil conquer you, but conquer evil by doing good. **Romans 12:19-21**

When we as humans seek revenge against another person, it almost always stems from unrighteous anger and hatred. Although God is not a "mean" God, as many may misconceive, He *does* get angry at the enemy, sin, evil, and injustice. God calls us to entrust *Him* with the "payback" and instead focus on loving those who wrong us. Are you trying to take revenge on someone right now whom God intended to receive your love instead?

God, You are love, and Your perspective of us is not one of disappointment, but of desire for a relationship. We receive Your love into our hearts and ask that You give us the discipline to let that love flow through us into others...even the unlovable. In Jesus' name we pray this.

13
INFLUENCE

Influence is built and utilized by following Jesus. The focus of this session is to discuss how influence is established by obeying God's Word.

Jesus is *the* Influencer of influencers.

I also pray that you will understand the incredible greatness of God's power for us who believe Him. This is the same mighty power that raised Christ from the dead and seated Him in the place of honor at God's right hand in the heavenly realms. Now He is far above any ruler or authority or power or leader or anything else—not only in this world but also in the world to come. God has put all things under the authority of Christ and has made Him head over all things for the benefit of the church. And the church is His body; it is made full and complete by Christ, who fills all things everywhere with Himself. **Ephesians 1:19-23**

Jesus has influence over anything and everything. You name it, He is over it. What are some of the dominant influences in culture that are under Jesus' authority but often loom in our hearts as more powerful? Who are some of the impressive "influencers" that will one day bow their knees to Jesus?

God's influence *and* the influence He endowed to us as humans, is incomprehensible.

When I look at the night sky and see the work of Your fingers—the moon and the stars You set in place—what are mere mortals that You should think about them, human beings that You should care for them? Yet You made them only a little lower than God and crowned them with glory and honor. You gave them charge of everything You made, putting all things under their authority... **Psalm 8:3-6**

Our Creator is so powerful and holy that it is comical for us to think we deserve anything from Him. Yet, God "gave [us] charge of everything [He] made." We have been privileged with platforms and positions for one purpose—pointing to King Jesus. What divine influence has God allowed us to have that we are taking for granted at this point in life? Who is around us that needs to be influenced for Jesus?

Influence is not self-acquired, but God-granted.

[Jabez] was the one who prayed to the God of Israel, "Oh, that you would bless me and expand my territory! Please be with me in all that I do, and keep me from all trouble and pain!" And God granted him his request. **1 Chronicles 4:10**

Jabez, who was "more honorable than any of his brothers," sets a precedent for us as warriors by acknowledging that it is *God* who gives us influence. We tend to base influence off of *our* progress, intelligence, hard work, and accomplishments, but self-manufactured impact is frail. What specific territory are we asking God to give us for His Kingdom? And are we asking God to bless us for *our* benefit or so that we can honor Him by blessing others?

Influence comes from pleasing God, not man.

Obviously, I'm not trying to win the approval of people, but of God. If pleasing people were my goal, I would not be Christ's servant. **Galatians 1:10**

A life lived for God will often translate to a life that disappoints man. In fact, if we desire to appease man, we literally cannot be a disciple of Jesus. Have you ever let someone down or hurt them simply by obeying God?

Being compassionate is how we influence others most effectively.

...All of you should be of one mind. Sympathize with each other. Love each other as brothers and sisters. Be tenderhearted, and keep a humble attitude. **1 Peter 3:8**

In 1 Corinthians 9:22, Paul encourages us to "share [the] weakness" of the weak and "find common ground with everyone" so that we can "save some." Influence identifies and sympathizes with, and even tries to relieve the pain and concerns of, others even if their experiences are not completely relatable or understood. Where (and with whom) do you struggle to be tenderhearted and empathetic?

Godly influence emerges from humble self-awareness of our unworthiness.

This is a trustworthy saying, and everyone should accept it: "Christ Jesus came into the world to save sinners"—and I am the worst of them all. But God had mercy on me so that Christ Jesus could use me as a prime example of His great patience with even the worst sinners. Then others will realize that they, too, can believe in Him and receive eternal life. **1 Timothy 1:15-16**

In this passage, Paul exhibits the kind of pride-destroying mentality we as warriors must have. Lucifer, our spiritual enemy, was expelled from heaven because of *pride.* To an extent, we all as men are Lucifer. Deep down, we want it to be about us. We want to be our god. We want the worship. We want the attention. We want to be the leader. We want to be the alpha. We want to be number one. And we sure don't like being second to the next guy. This is our problem—we don't want to be in another man's shadow. But the ultimate test of manhood is to be in another Man's shadow. We should have one goal in our influence—to be eclipsed by Jesus. Do we have any areas where pride or a mistaken sense of worthiness is restricting influence for Jesus? At the end of the day, do we see ourselves as impressive or unimpressive apart from Jesus' partnership?

Warriors passionately influence their families to live for Jesus.

Direct your children onto the right path, and when they are older, they will not leave it. **Proverbs 22:6**

If we want to be a worthwhile influencer, we will accurately reflect Jesus for our families and point them to God's Word again and again. How do we feed our families with God's Word and fight for God's presence in our homes on a daily basis?

God, thank You for granting us supernatural influence through the power of Your Son, Your Holy Spirit, and Your Word. Help us to recognize *why* You give us influence—to point others to You—and to be, first and foremost, compassionate, as we develop relationships with others. In Jesus' name we pray this.

14
FOCUS

Tenacious focus is crucial for spiritual victory. The focus of this session is to discuss what the Word says about remaining fixated on Jesus and on eternity.

A warrior's big-picture focus is not on his temporary residence, but his permanent home.

Since you have been raised to new life with Christ, set your sights on the realities of heaven, where Christ sits in the place of honor at God's right hand. Think about the things of heaven, not the things of earth. **Colossians 3:1-2**

Keeping our macro focus set on something we have yet to experience is extremely difficult because of the allure of the place we are currently experiencing. We will discuss the "realities of heaven" later in this study, but why is it so effortless to think about the things of earth instead of the things of heaven?

A warrior's moment-by-moment focus is on fighting in Jesus' victory against a relentless enemy.

Stay alert! Watch out for your great enemy, the devil. He prowls around like a roaring lion, looking for someone to devour. **1 Peter 5:8**

The spiritual battle never stops because the enemy never rests. He ceaselessly circles us and studies us, usually watching for a moment of isolation to attack. Notice how he is looking for "someone"—not two or three, but *one*—to destroy. How does staying connected daily to other warriors help us stay alert and aware of the enemy's stealthy tactics?

Warriors focus on exercising God's power to escape temptation.

If you think you are standing strong, be careful not to fall. The temptations in your life are no different from what others experience. And God is faithful. He will not allow the temptation to be more than you can stand. When you are tempted, He will show you a way out so that you can endure. **1 Corinthians 10:12-13**

Every man in the history of the world has faced the same temptations. The men who defeat those temptations are the men who maintain an obsessive focus on the power of Jesus in them. The way out is *always* through the power of Christ and His Word. When temptation comes, how do we actually *use* the supernatural power available to us? What does this look like and how does voicing scripture and the name of Jesus give us inexplicable, undefiable domination over sin?

Our aim every day is to decrease so that Jesus can increase.

He must become greater and greater, and I must become less and less. **John 3:30**

Peace comes from subtraction, not addition. When we become less, Jesus becomes more, and as a result, our peace become greater. Is there any worldly focus right now that needs to be subtracted so that God's presence can be multiplied?

Our focus during difficulty is the peace and victory of Jesus.

[Jesus said to His disciples,] "But the time is coming—indeed it's here now—when you will be scattered, each one going his own way, leaving Me alone. Yet I am not alone because the Father is with Me. I have told you all this so that you may have peace in Me. Here on earth you will have many trials and sorrows. But take heart, because I have overcome the world." **John 16:33-34**

Challenges in life are guaranteed. Jesus said so. But peace and victory *during* those challenges are also guaranteed if we align our thoughts and actions with Jesus' commands. Because Jesus has overcome the world, we can have peace. Is there a situation right now in your life that seems to be lacking peace and victory? Are you standing obediently until victory emerges from the darkness and uncertainty?

Warriors are focused on *going* and *telling* others about Jesus.

"Men of Galilee," [the white-robed men] said, "why are you standing here staring into heaven? Jesus has been taken from you into heaven, but someday He will return from heaven in the same way you saw Him go!" **Acts 1:11**

When Jesus ascended into heaven after His resurrection from the grave, the disciples were baffled. Two angels appeared and essentially said, "Stop standing and staring and *go tell* others about Jesus' return!" How are we going and telling others *outside* of the church about the fact that Jesus is going to come back to "bring salvation to all who are eagerly waiting for Him" (Hebrews 9:28)?

Warriors are aware that Jesus' return could come at any second.

...A day is like a thousand years to the Lord, and a thousand years is like a day. The Lord isn't really being slow about His promise...No, He is being patient for your sake. He does not want anyone to be destroyed, but wants everyone to repent. But the day of the Lord will come as unexpectedly as a thief. Then the heavens will pass away with a terrible noise, and the very elements themselves will disappear in fire, and the earth and everything on it will be found to deserve judgment. **2 Peter 3:8-10**

If Jesus returned right now, would you be able to say you did all you could do to bring your family and the circle of people around you to Jesus while on this earth? What practical steps is God calling you to take to accomplish His mission? Is it leading other men in a Bible study? Is it leading a small group with your wife? Is it using your time and talent to serve the church?

Our perspective is set on the *privilege* of being called as warriors for Jesus.

If you are insulted because you bear the name of Christ, you will be blessed, for the glorious Spirit of God rests upon you...But it is no shame to suffer for being a Christian. Praise God for the privilege of being called by His name! **1 Peter 4:14,16**

There is no shame in suffering for serving the living Christ. Honestly, do we consider it a burden or an honor to be one of Jesus' men?

God, Your glory is our focus. Jesus is our focus. Heaven and eternity are our focus. The lost are our focus. Let us not just profess these things, but actually *live* them. Give us an untiring, unwavering fixation on Your mission. In Jesus' name we pray this.

15
THOUGHTS & ACTIONS

The mind is the battlefield of spiritual war. The focus of this session is to discuss how thinking like Jesus leads us to acting like Jesus.

To to change how we act, we must first let God change the way we think.

*Don't copy the behavior and customs of this world, but let God transform you into a new person by changing the way you think. Then you will learn to know God's will for you, which is good and pleasing and perfect. **Romans 12:2***

Thoughts establish actions. If we want to *act* like Jesus, it starts with *thinking* like Jesus. This is a process that only God can initiate. Second Corinthians 5:17 tells us that "anyone who belongs to Christ has become a *new* person." God does not want to just improve our thought life; He wants to *transform* it into something completely new. "Transform" comes from the Greek "metamorphoo," where we get the word "metamorphosis." When a caterpillar changes into a butterfly, it is a *complete* transfiguration from the inside out. The work God wants to do in us takes time and can be messy, but the end result is beautiful if we let Him overhaul our thinking. How do our thoughts shift when God transforms our minds?

Spiritual victory begins with obedience of our thoughts.

*We are human, but we don't wage war as humans do. We use God's mighty weapons, not worldly weapons, to knock down the strongholds of human reasoning and to destroy false arguments. We destroy every proud obstacle that keeps people from knowing God. We capture their rebellious thoughts and teach them to obey Christ. **2 Corinthians 10:3-5***

Spiritual war is one that is fought in the mind, between truth and lies. With each thought that enters, we must take it into captivity and let God distinguish what is righteous from what is unrighteous. The Greek etymology of the word "captive," used in this passage, is "aichmalotizo," which literally means "to be captured" or "brought into subjection" by using "a spear." So, taking a thought captive means we set up an armed security checkpoint at the front gate of our minds. And when any thought approaches the entrance, it is aggressively confronted and paused for examination before it goes any further. Then we stick the point of a spear up to that thought's neck and lead it immediately over to the Judge's seat before it is permitted to infiltrate our intellect. And if the Holy Spirit reveals to us that He doesn't like it, we instantaneously execute that thought by piercing it with the razor-sharp head of that spear! Are we engaging in this level of spiritual warfare to protect our minds and preserve victory?

Spirit-led thoughts bring life; sin-led thoughts bring death.

*Those who are dominated by the sinful nature think about sinful things, but those who are controlled by the Holy Spirit think about things that please the Spirit. So letting your sinful nature control your mind leads to death. But letting the Spirit control your mind leads to life and peace. **Romans 8:5-6***

We as men tend to compartmentalize our lives. We section off our lives and will often partition off certain areas (or even environments) from God. We are okay with God controlling our Sunday behavior at church, but not our Thursday morning thoughts at the office or Friday night habits in the neighborhood. Are there any compartments in our lives that are still pockets for sin-led living instead of Spirit-led living?

The enemy opportunistically targets our weakest moments to attack.

When the devil had finished tempting Jesus, he left Him until the next opportunity came. **Luke 4:13**

Part of Satan's conniving character is his patient intelligence. He waits for our most vulnerable moments to steal our purity and peace. We must be on guard. What seasons or times of day do we seem to be at our weakest in our thought life? What triggers usually accompany those weak moments? Exhaustion? Finances? Pleasure?

Our eyes are an entrance to our thoughts.

[Jesus said,] "Your eye is like a lamp that provides light for your body. When your eye is healthy, your whole body is filled with light. But when your eye is unhealthy, your whole body is filled with darkness..." **Matthew 6:22-23**

What we *see* has immeasurable impact on our spiritual health, escorting light or dark into our thoughts. Are there any situations or inlets that always seem to bring darkness into our bodies through the eyes and ears? And how can we counter those situations or inlets with replacement influences that would bring light in instead?

Peace of mind comes from eyes set on Jesus.

You will keep in perfect peace all who trust in You, all whose thoughts are fixed on You! **Isaiah 26:3**

How often do we turn on worship music, close our eyes, and *see* Jesus' blood-drenched cross and vacant tomb with our mind's eye? How does conceiving that imagery and recollecting those scenes bring peace to our perspective?

God's thoughts are laughably wiser than ours.

"My thoughts are nothing like your thoughts," says the Lord. "And My ways are far beyond anything you could imagine. For just as the heavens are higher than the earth, so My ways are higher than your ways and My thoughts higher than your thoughts." **Isaiah 55:8-9**

So often, we wonder why God is allowing difficulty and pain into our circumstances. We must recognize that He sees what we don't and He knows far more than we do. We can't comprehend the perfection of the mind of God. What circumstance of yours needs reminding right now that God does everything for our good and for His glory?

Actions of boys are dictated by emotions, actions of men by principles.

The commandments of the Lord are right, bringing joy to the heart. **Psalm 19:8**

Pastor Chris Hodges often says this: "Choices lead. Feelings follow." Are we disciplined enough to act on God's Word when we don't feel like it?

God, our minds are the decisive territory of spiritual warfare. We recognize that we cannot *act* like Jesus until we *think* like Jesus. We ask Your Holy Spirit to transform our thoughts to become like Your Son's. In Jesus' name we pray this.

16
FORGIVENESS

Forgiveness is the cornerstone of Jesus. The focus of this session is to discuss what the Word says about the necessity and power of God's forgiveness in us and through us.

God forgives us and heals us.

Let all that I am praise the Lord; may I never forget the good things He does for me. He forgives all my sins and heals all my diseases. **Psalm 103:2-3**

Through the sacrifice of His Son, Jesus Christ, God bought forgiveness and healing for those that believe in Him. This changes everything because it means God has power over both forces that lead to death—sin and sickness. While confession does not guarantee physical healing on earth, being right with God promises ultimate healing for eternity. In what ways does receiving God's forgiveness bring us healing?

Confession brings forgiveness. Forgiveness brings freedom.

Finally, I confessed all my sins to You and stopped trying to hide my guilt. I said to myself, "I will confess my rebellion to the Lord." And You forgave me! All my guilt is gone. **Psalm 32:5**

Confession is to agree with God that what we did was sin. His full and free forgiveness comes from Jesus' blood alone. This doesn't give us a license to sin but rather motivates us to walk in freedom. God's forgiveness of every sin we have ever committed or will ever commit is a miracle. God wants to exchange the guilt, shame, and regret of our sin and release us into peace and freedom. Not to mention, God tells us in Isaiah 43:25, "I—yes, I alone—will blot out your sins for my own sake and will *never* think of them again." Incredible. God overwhelms us with His goodness and forgets our badness. Who can attest to the peace and freedom that God's forgiveness brings?

God's forgiveness is undeservedly tenderhearted and thorough.

The Lord is compassionate and merciful, slow to get angry and filled with unfailing love...He does not punish us for all our sins; He does not deal harshly with us, as we deserve. For His unfailing love toward those who fear Him is as great as the height of the heavens above the earth. He has removed our sins as far from us as the east is from the west. **Psalm 103:8,10-12**

When we confess, God's forgiveness is not partial to recipient or to sin. We are *all* candidates for forgiveness, and *all* sin is eradicated by the blood of Jesus. Jesus' blood is the infallible sanitizing agent for all who repent and believe in the Gospel of Jesus. And once sin is gone, it's gone. What mistakes in our past need to be reminded of their *permanent* removal from our record?

Repentance brings refreshment.

Now repent of your sins and turn to God, so that your sins may be wiped away. Then times of refreshment will come from the presence of the Lord... **Acts 3:19-20**

God is quick to forgive when we turn from sin to Him. That shift in our direction shows that we are serious about obedience. God's forgiveness is instantaneous and complete, and He blesses repentance by refreshing us. What is the most refreshing thing you've ever experienced? Was it a walk on a beach? Was it a cold drink on a hot day? Was it a hobby you enjoyed? How did it make you feel? How are those feelings similar to being in God's presence?

Forgiveness neutralizes hatred.

Get rid of all bitterness, rage, anger, harsh words, and slander, as well as all types of evil behavior. Instead, be kind to each other, tenderhearted, forgiving one another, just as God through Christ has forgiven you. **Ephesians 4:31-32**

Forgiveness is a deliberate *choice* to release someone from every fruit of our frustration toward them, whether they deserve it or not. We make this disciplined choice because God forgave us first and paid the highest price to do so. And when we release someone else from our bitterness and anger, God supernaturally intervenes and releases *us*. By forgiving, the offended are freed. Are we carrying any emotional baggage caused by a father, mother, spouse, sibling, or rival that needs to be unloaded? Who do we need to forgive right now?

Forgiveness has no quota.

[Jesus said,] "Even if [a] person wrongs you seven times a day and each time turns again and asks forgiveness, you must forgive." **Luke 17:4**

This principle is exasperating for our flesh. Jesus tells us there is no limit to the number of times we should forgive someone. Ouch. Talk about a difficult command. But isn't that exactly what Jesus modeled for us during His crucifixion? Nail after nail, lash after lash...Jesus' forgiveness was limitless. In no way is constant abuse in a relationship warranted, but continual forgiveness always is. Is there anyone who hurt us so many times that we now have justified not forgiving them?

We let others off the hook before they're even on it.

Make allowance for each other's faults, and forgive anyone who offends you. Remember, the Lord forgave you, so you must forgive others. **Colossians 3:13**

The most effective way to forgive is to pre-pardon the offender before they've even made a mistake. Maintaining generous margin for other's faults allows us to walk baggage-free through life. How is the Holy Spirit crucial to living this way?

If we want to receive forgiveness, we must offer forgiveness.

[Jesus said,] "If you forgive those who sin against you, your heavenly Father will forgive you. But if you refuse to forgive others, your Father will not forgive your sins." **Matthew 6:14-15**

Jesus is crystal clear in telling us that God forgives only those who forgive. Extending forgiveness is essentially proof that we know God. How can following our feelings toward others jeopardize our eligibility for God's best in our lives?

God, Your forgiveness is so undeserved. Thank You for releasing us from Your anger and paying the price for our sins with Your Son's blood. Now let us be conduits of Your forgiveness and choose to release others from *our* frustration and bitterness. Holy Spirit, fill us, because only You can make this possible. In Jesus' name we pray this.

17
COMMUNICATION

All relationships are formed and shaped by communication. The focus of this session is to discuss the significance of obedience in communicating with God and others.

Sin and disobedience block our communication with God, hindering His blessings.

"Since they refused to listen when I called to them, I would not listen when they called to Me, says the Lord of Heaven's Armies." Zechariah 7:13

In His Word, God gives us many conditional promises—"*If* you do this, *then* I will do that." One of those promises is that He listens *if* we listen. God *hears* all prayers, but He only *responds* to the prayers of those who acknowledge Jesus as their Savior and whose lives are in alignment with Jesus as their Lord. When we do not heed God's communication, He does not respond to ours. That means our prayers are more effective when sin is absent. This may be best suited as a rhetorical question, but is there any area of sin that could be impeding God's response to your prayers?

Obedience assures God's responsiveness to our communication.

The eyes of the Lord watch over those who do right; His ears are open to their cries for help. But the Lord turns His face against those who do evil... Psalm 34:15-16

The presence of sin in our lives inhibits God's response to our prayers, but obedience *attracts* God's favor. John 9:31 illustrates this contrast, as a blind man just healed by Jesus says, "We know that God doesn't listen to sinners, but He is ready to hear those who worship Him and do His will." Both for believers *and* unbelievers, a repentant heart and a desire to obey Jesus are what optimize the communication line between us and God. Wouldn't it be inconsistent with God's holy nature for Him to honor the requests of people living unholy lives?

Wise communication heals, not hurts.

Some people make cutting remarks, but the words of the wise bring healing. Proverbs 12:18

In most disagreements, it makes us feel better in the moment to just "tell it like it is"—a.k.a. hurl a hurtful comment in someone else's face. How does pride lead to hurting instead of healing? Why do we naturally want to hurt those that hurt us?

The fewer the words, the wiser the man.

A truly wise person uses few words; a person with understanding is even-tempered. Even fools are thought wise when they keep silent; with their mouths shut, they seem intelligent. Proverbs 17:27-28

God's Word encourages us to "use few words" and to literally "shut [our] mouths" if we want to exercise wisdom and restraint. Proverbs 29:11 reiterates that "fools vent their anger, but the wise quietly hold it back." In what situations would we be wise to "keep silent" the next time they occur?

A warrior is a gentle communicator.

A gentle answer deflects anger, but harsh words make tempers flare. **Proverbs 15:1**

Gentleness *always* de-escalates conflict. What moments in our lives tend to feature heated arguments and attempts to "pour salt in open wounds"? How does gentleness help us protect the insecurities of others instead of exposing them?

Our communication simply matches our actions.

Just say a simple, 'Yes, I will,' or 'No, I won't.' Anything beyond this is from the evil one. **Matthew 5:37**

What a warrior says, a warrior does. A simple verbal commitment is an agreement that binds our words and actions. Who is the most reliable man of God in your life? Does their communication ever involve exaggeration or extra emphasis, or do their simple "yes" and "no" suffice?

A warrior communicates often to his wife that she is a treasure.

The man who finds a wife finds a treasure, and he receives favor from the Lord. **Proverbs 18:22**

God defines our wives as treasures. Our wives need to hear this truth communicated from their husbands. How does uplifting communication build a healthy marriage and household?

Our communication with unbelievers is not forceful or judgmental, but patient and graceful.

Live wisely among those who are not believers, and make the most of every opportunity. Let your conversation be gracious and attractive so that you will have the right response for everyone. **Colossians 4:5-6**

We can point others to Christ by the way we communicate. Our *love* for non-believers creates the opportunity for us to share truth with them. As the saying from Theodore Roosevelt goes, "No one cares how much you know, until they know how much you care." Relationship precedes reproof. Are our countenance and communication with the lost attractive or repulsive? How can we be sure our words make unbelievers want *more* of what we have, not less?

Because Jesus has experienced it all, He can help us through it all.

Since [Jesus] Himself has gone through suffering and testing, He is able to help us when we are being tested. **Hebrews 2:18**

Does our communication with Jesus consider and honor the profound wisdom He has as a human who already passed every test we face?

God, our world is built by communication, and we desperately need more of Your Truth to mold the way we speak and the way we live. Since the beginning, the enemy has lied, confused, and misconstrued in his plot to divide us and destroy us. Give us Spirit-led freedom from pride and deception as we interact with others, and let our communication be loving, gentle, gracious, and healing. In Jesus' name we pray this.

18
MONEY

Our perspective and stewardship of money is critical to spiritual victory. The focus of this session is to discuss what the Word says about our approach toward money.

Money is a resource to serve people and spread the Gospel.

*[Jesus said,] "No one can serve two masters. For you will hate one and love the other; you will be devoted to one and despise the other. You cannot serve God and be enslaved to money." **Matthew 6:24***

Money is god-like. The spirit of "mammon"—material riches—holds tremendous power. After all, it can give us just about anything we want here on earth except for physical healing. With enough money, you can go anywhere and buy anything... sadly, even a spouse, if the price is right. But while money might buy a spouse, it can never buy true love, fulfillment, and satisfaction. Money used to advance the Gospel is the only money that can truly fulfill. How can utilizing money as a *resource* to point people to Jesus *protect* every dollar from having an unrighteous spirit on it?

Obsessing over money will devastate your life and deteriorate your peace.

*For the love of money is the root of all kinds of evil. And some people, craving money, have wandered from the true faith and pierced themselves with many sorrows. **1 Timothy 6:10***

Money isn't evil. It is a necessary resource. However, when we *love* money, it sprouts "all kinds of evil." Making money can be intoxicating. If you've ever had money in the stock market, you know how tightly money can grip your mind and emotions. It is overwhelming. Has there ever been a time in your life where you "craved money" and let money temporarily become your god? What are some of the "sorrows" that "pierce" us when we are motivated by money?

Warriors *live* like money cannot bring peace.

*Those who love money will never have enough. How meaningless to think that wealth brings true happiness! **Ecclesiastes 5:10***

It is one thing to know something, but a completely different challenge to live it. We *know* that money cannot buy the peace or contentment that we crave, but it sure doesn't stop us from trying to accumulate wealth. What do we truly envision as the end goal for money? Is it security? Control? Comfort? Luxury? Status? Why do we try to fight the truth of Psalm 107:9—that only Jesus "satisfies the thirsty and fills the hungry with good things"?

When we give God our first, He blesses the remainder.

*Honor the Lord with your wealth and with the best part of everything you produce. Then He will fill your barns with grain, and your vats will overflow with good wine. **Proverbs 3:9-10***

Our best is our first. This can be applied to money, time, energy, and every other asset we have to invest in life. What is God's "money-back guarantee" when we give the first of everything to Him by investing in His church? And how does tithing ensure that money remains dethroned from being the god of our hearts?

Giving the tithe—one-tenth of what we produce—*back* to God is a priority.

One-tenth of the produce of the land, whether grain from the fields or fruit from the trees, belongs to the Lord and must be set apart to Him as holy. **Leviticus 27:30**

God tells us in Psalm 50:12, "all the world is Mine and everything in it." Job 1:21 reminds us that "the Lord gave [us] what [we have]." Considering these two truths, even if the New Testament does not specifically address tithing (10% precisely), shouldn't we be delighted to give *back* a small portion of what God has given to us? If we are brutally honest, is it *fear* of not having enough money that justifies our unwillingness to tithe? Or is it *greed* for more money that tempts us not to tithe?

Our priority is pleasing the Provider, not attaining the provision.

Trust in your money and down you go! But the godly flourish like leaves in spring. **Proverbs 11:28**

God calls us to work hard to pay the bills and put food on the table for our families, but that is not the top priority. God wants our primary focus on obeying His Word, assuring us in Proverbs 10:3 that "[He] will not let the godly go hungry." Has there ever been a dry season financially when God could have actually been testing your obedience, not your work ethic?

Wise money management saves more, spends less, and avoids debt.

The wise have wealth and luxury, but fools spend whatever they get. **Proverbs 21:20**

Those with more than enough in their bank accounts are not necessarily those who *make more* money. However, they are usually the ones who *spend less* money. Wise money managers adhere to Proverbs 22:7: "Just as the rich rule the poor, so the borrower is servant to the lender." Out-of-control spending inevitably accumulates debt. Debt ensures bondage. Are we disciplined enough to say "no" to instant gratification and appreciate the compounding effect of saving even pennies over time? When we spend money, are we purchasing a product or a feeling?

Investing in others invigorates us.

The generous will prosper; those who refresh others will themselves be refreshed. **Proverbs 11:25**

Generosity energizes us. In the words of Jesus from Acts 20:35, "It is more blessed to give than to receive." And the imprint we leave on this earth will not be measured by what we *get*, but what we *give*. Do you have an example of a time when you were "refreshed" by generously giving your time, talents, and resources to someone else?

God, everything, including money, belongs to You. You own it all. Let us glorify You with every dollar You allow us to steward. We joyfully give You our first by investing in Your church, and we ask that You point out opportunities to bless others with our generosity. We acknowledge that money is a wonderful resource, but an incompetent god. Let us use it to build Your Kingdom, not ours. In Jesus' name we pray this.

19
MARGIN

Margin maximizes our effectiveness as warriors for Jesus. The focus of this session is to discuss what the Word says about the discipline of establishing and utilizing margin for Jesus.

Margin is a byproduct of placing God as the priority.

Seek the Kingdom of God above all else, and live righteously, and He will give you everything you need. **Matthew 6:33**

Margin is crucial to spiritual health. It is the surplus—the reserve, or buffer—that gives us breathing room to face life's challenges most efficiently. Whether it is physical, financial, emotional, mental, or relational, margin begins with nurturing our *spiritual* health first. In what area of life would you most like some more margin?

Relational margin—daily time in God's presence—is our first priority.

Before daybreak the next morning, Jesus got up and went out to an isolated place to pray. **Mark 1:35**

If we want to be like Jesus, we will create margin with our *time* at the *beginning* of each day to spend with God. Warriors *make* the time for this discipline of carving out space in our schedule, and it yields huge dividends. How does the *morning* time establish the complexion of each day? How does "[being still] and [knowing] that [God] is God" allow Him to chart the correct course for every day?

Rest optimizes performance by replenishing margin.

Using a dull ax requires great strength, so sharpen the blade. That's the value of wisdom; it helps you succeed. **Ecclesiastes 10:10**

Physical and spiritual rest both help to "sharpen [our] blade[s]." Warriors show wisdom when we mandate rest in our routine. Rest establishes margin by enhancing our presence. When our tanks are filled and overflowing, we offer far more value to those around us. Are we in a habit of taking one day each week (as God demonstrated to us after creating the universe) to rest our bodies and minds as our spirits reflect on God's greatness? What does your Sabbath routine look like?

Chasing worldly gods exhausts us and prevents margin.

[The Lord said,] "When will you stop running? When will you stop panting after other gods?..." **Jeremiah 2:25**

Exhaustion, stress, anxiety, and worry often come during times when we're chasing worldly gods. We obsess over accumulating more money, building our popularity, or enjoying life's pleasures, and we are left "panting" from worthless exertion. What "foreign gods" are we "running" after that are tiring us out?

Physical margin nurtures the fruits of the Holy Spirit.

But the Holy Spirit produces this kind of fruit in our lives: love, joy, peace, patience, kindness, goodness, faithfulness, gentleness, and self-control... **Galatians 5:22-23**

When we operate in God's strength, we burn in the power of the Spirit, but when we operate in our own strength, we burn out. Physical and spiritual fatigue will almost certainly stifle spiritual fruit. When we are worn down and sleep-deprived, conditions are unfavorable to produce the attributes of Jesus in our lives. Which of these "fruits of the Spirit" seem to suffer most when you are exhausted?

Gospel-driven generosity generates margin.

Give freely and become more wealthy; be stingy and lose everything. **Proverbs 11:24**

The concept of building wealth is usually associated with *getting*, but God's Word tells us that His surplus on our estate actually comes from *giving*. God always replenishes the supply of the generous. What are some ways we can give to others while giving them the Gospel? How can we meet a practical need while sowing an eternal seed?

God promises margin when we tithe our income.

"Bring all the tithes into the storehouse so there will be enough food in My Temple. If you do," says the Lord of Heaven's Armies, "I will open the windows of heaven for you. I will pour out a blessing so great you won't have enough room to take it in! Try it! Put Me to the test!" **Malachi 3:10**

God guarantees overwhelming blessings in response to our financial faithfulness. He even says, "Try me, and just watch." Far beyond financial gain, God blesses us with the spiritual excess of peace, joy, and satisfaction in Him no matter how much money we have. Who can testify to the supernatural power of tithing to God's church? Do we believe that God's blessing over 90% of our money will yield far more than our management of 100% of our money?

Integrity, patience, and hard work build sustainable financial margin.

Wealth from get-rich-quick schemes quickly disappears; wealth from hard work grows over time. **Proverbs 13:11**

Warriors work honestly, patiently, and diligently to build wealth. We don't live in a fantasy world, lazily and foolishly hoping that one day we'll win the lottery or hit it big on a pyramid scheme. What are some ways to build financial margin over time?

Margin is found in offloading our burdens on Jesus.

Then Jesus said, "Come to Me, all of you who are weary and carry heavy burdens, and I will give you rest. Take My yoke upon you. Let Me teach you, because I am humble and gentle at heart, and you will find rest for your souls." **Matthew 11:28-29**

Trying to carry our burdens instead of simply praying about them will wear us out. Rest is found only in the finished work of the cross. What kind of burden—financial, relational, physical, mental, emotional, or even professional—do you tend to wear the most? How does connecting with the cross of Jesus in worship give us true rest?

God, You are our priority. We seek You and Your Kingdom first, certain that You will provide over and beyond for our needs in every area of life. You are the source of margin, so supply us with supernatural rest and every resource needed to advance Your Gospel. In Jesus' name we pray this.

20
STEWARDSHIP

God calls us to steward His provision for His purpose. The focus of this session is to discuss what the Word says about managing and leveraging resources for eternity.

Everything we have is a gift from God to steward for His purpose.

...What do you have that God hasn't given you? And if everything you have is from God, why boast as though it were not a gift? **1 Corinthians 4:7**

Whatever we have, even if we worked hard to attain it, came to us because God allowed it. God owns it all. As Psalm 50:10 says, He "own[s] the cattle on a thousand hills." And He desires for us to have things for one reason—to connect people to Jesus. Are there any accomplishments, belongings, or talents that we mistakenly take credit for attaining?

We either view money and possessions as resources or gods.

[Jesus said,] "Here's the lesson: Use your worldly resources to benefit others and make friends. Then, when your possessions are gone, they will welcome you to an eternal home. If you are faithful in little things, you will be faithful in large ones. But if you are dishonest in little things, you won't be honest with greater responsibilities. And if you are untrustworthy about worldly wealth, who will trust you with the true riches of heaven?" **Luke 16:9-11**

Money and possessions come from God. In and of themselves, they are good things... as long as we treat them as resources to reach people for eternity, not golden tickets to our earthly dreams. How can we maximize our eternal return on investment with our earthly possessions? How can we utilize our bank accounts, houses, vehicles, and more to bring others the Gospel?

Riches are worthless without a relationship with Jesus.

[Jesus said,] "Yes, a person is a fool to store up earthly wealth but not have a rich relationship with God." **Luke 12:21**

Matthew 6:19-20 urges, "Don't store up treasures here on earth," where they deteriorate and decay, but to "store [our] treasures in heaven," where they last forever. Worthwhile stewardship is driven by giving *Jesus* to people, not just giving them *things* that will rot away over time. Even philanthropic efforts that do not include the Gospel are eternally irrelevant. That said, why is it still essential that we meet a practical need as we share Jesus with someone?

Stewardship is not about showmanship.

[Jesus said,] "But when you give to someone in need, don't let your left hand know what your right hand is doing. Give your gifts in private, and your Father, who sees everything, will reward you." **Matthew 6:3-4**

God's stance on the spotlight is consistent in Scripture—it is for *Him*, not us. We don't gloat when we give. Why is it gratifying, even intoxicating, to be noticed and commended for our generosity?

Generosity is about the attitude of the heart, not just the amount of the gift.

Remember this—a farmer who plants only a few seeds will get a small crop. But the one who plants generously will get a generous crop. You must each decide in your heart how much to give. And don't give reluctantly or in response to pressure. "For God loves a person who gives cheerfully." And God will generously provide all you need. Then you will always have everything you need and plenty left over to share with others. **2 Corinthians 9:6-8**

The more seed we sow, the more harvest we reap. God often gives back to us in ways far more valuable than money. Regardless, the *amount* we give is not what God cares about most. He is watching the *spirit* with which we sow. Do we sigh or sulk when we give, considering it an inconvenience? Or do we smile, celebrating it as an honor?

The more we give, the more we will receive.

[Jesus said,] "Give, and you will receive. Your gift will return to you in full—pressed down, shaken together to make room for more, running over, and poured into your lap. The amount you give will determine the amount you get back." **Luke 6:38**

We don't give to get, but God promises that getting more *is* an effect of giving with the right motive. Have you ever seen this promise proven before your eyes, where God saw your giving time, talents, and resources, and raised His blessings back to you?

God has wired us with talents to serve people and draw them to Him.

In His grace, God has given us different gifts for doing certain things well. So if God has given you the ability to prophesy, speak out with as much faith as God has given you. If your gift is serving others, serve them well. If you are a teacher, teach well. If your gift is to encourage others, be encouraging. If it is giving, give generously. If God has given you leadership ability, take the responsibility seriously. And if you have a gift for showing kindness to others, do it gladly. **Romans 12:6-8**

God cares not only about the stewardship of our money but of *all* our resources, including time, talents, and possessions. What skills and strengths do you believe God has given you to serve His church? Do you have an experience in which "God's mighty power at work within [you]...accomplish[ed] infinitely more" than you thought was possible after stepping out in obedience to God, as Ephesians 3:20 promises?

Stewardship aims for the "well done" from Jesus.

"The master said, 'Well done, my good and faithful servant. You have been faithful in handling this small amount, so now I will give you many more responsibilities. Let's celebrate together!'" **Matthew 25:23**

Second Corinthians 5:10 tells us that we will one day face Jesus and He will look at the fruit that our faith produced while we were on earth. There is no higher honor than being told by the King Himself that we did a great job. How are our worship encounters with Jesus moving us to action to receive the "well done"? Practically, what are we *doing* to tell others the life-changing truth?

God, there is intentionality behind every dollar, possession, and talent You entrust to us. Help us not to squander Your resources or waste them on ourselves, but instead to pinpoint opportunities to get creative in using Your provision to connect others to You. In Jesus' name we pray this.

21
EXCELLENCE

Excellence is the default standard for warriors. The focus of this session is to discuss what the Word says about reflecting God's nature by setting ourselves apart from the world.

God's version of my life is the most excellent version of my life.

The Lord says, "I will guide you along the best pathway for your life. I will advise you and watch over you." **Psalm 32:8**

We are deceived if we believe there is a more abundant, peace-filled path for our lives than God's. It is indisputable—obedience maximizes abundance. As 1 John 5:12 puts it, "Whoever has the Son has life; whoever does not have God's Son does not have life." When we stay steadfast on absorbing Jesus' character and excelling as reflections of Him, it yields God's "best" by giving us "life." This means we can *relax* in obedience, even when circumstances seem frustrating or discouraging, because we are smack dab in the center of the version of life that we would prefer! How pivotal is it for us to voice confidence in the abundance of obedience during tough times?

God desires excellence and despises mediocrity.

"I know all the things you do, that you are neither hot nor cold. I wish that you were one or the other! But since you are like lukewarm water, neither hot nor cold, I will spit you out of my mouth!" **Revelation 3:15-16**

God wants us *on fire* for Him. We must fight to keep our flame from diminishing to a flicker. God's message to the mediocrity-plagued church in Laodicea gives us a glimpse of how much He despises lukewarmness. This passage goes on to cite *riches* as the origin of apathy. How do earthly comforts and luxuries corrode our enthusiasm for spiritual excellence?

Excellence for a warrior is an obsession with holiness.

So prepare your minds for action and exercise self-control...So you must live as God's obedient children. Don't slip back into your old ways of living to satisfy your own desires. You didn't know any better then. But now you must be holy in everything you do, just as God who chose you is holy. **1 Peter 1:13-15**

We are called by God to be holy—pure and set apart from the world. We do this by methodically eliminating sin from our lives. Living a holy life not only invigorates us, but it energizes us to excellence. How important is it for us to surround ourselves with standout men who value holiness and push us to excellence?

Sin stands in the way of excellence.

...Don't fool yourselves. Those who indulge in sexual sin, or who worship idols, or commit adultery, or are male prostitutes, or practice homosexuality, or are thieves, or greedy people, or drunkards, or are abusive, or cheat people—none of these will inherit the Kingdom of God. Some of you were once like that. But you were cleansed; you were made holy; you were made right with God by calling on the name of the Lord Jesus Christ and by the Spirit of our God. **1 Corinthians 6:9-11**

Hopefully, this passage is describing who we were before God saved us and set us apart for service, but God hates sin because it drives a wedge between us and His best. How do the worldly habits in this passage make us blend in with the majority?

We represent God with excellence in anything and everything we do.

So whether you eat or drink, or whatever you do, do it all for the glory of God. **1 Corinthians 10:31**

God's glory is the *why* behind "whatever [we] do," and Ecclesiastes 9:10 urges us to do everything "well." What are some everyday activities in your life in which you can glorify Jesus with excellence?

Excellence is established by enthusiasm.

So, my dear brothers and sisters, be strong and immovable. Always work enthusiastically for the Lord, for you know that nothing you do for the Lord is ever useless. **1 Corinthians 15:58**

Warriors are always focused on bringing our best to the table. We passionately build the sturdiest houses, coach the most disciplined teams, and balance the most accurate spreadsheets...all to point others to the excellence of Jesus for the glory of God. Who comes to mind when you think about the most enthusiastic leaders on the planet? How are the standout innovators, CEOs, and coaches obsessed with excellence in their respective fields? Would you agree that excellence affords influence?

When God grants us leadership, we honor Him by sharpening our skills.

[God] chose His servant David, calling him from the sheep pens. He took David from tending the ewes and lambs and made him the shepherd of Jacob's descendants—God's own people, Israel. He cared for them with a true heart and led them with skillful hands. **Psalm 78:70-72**

Honing our God-given skill sets honors our Creator and increases our influence for His Kingdom. Daniel 6:3 reiterates the impact of this principle, saying, "Because of Daniel's *great ability*, the king made plans to place him over the entire empire." What territory are you looking to impact for God's Kingdom by improving at your craft?

Discipline is the gateway to excellence.

No discipline is enjoyable while it is happening—it's painful! But afterward there will be a peaceful harvest of right living for those who are trained in this way. **Hebrews 12:11**

A critical component to reaping excellence in the future is denying our desires in the present. The Bible acknowledges that all discipline (including self-discipline) can be downright miserable while it is happening but that peace is produced as a result. Pastor Andy Stanley of North Point Community Church once said, "Giving up something now for something better later is not a sacrifice. It is an investment." Excellence can be a painful investment, but it maximizes God's potential in us. Who has an example of how enduring discomfort led to a later reward?

God, You are set apart and call us to be set apart, living lives of excellence in every way. Let us represent Your exceptional character in "whatever we do," and surround us with like-minded men who do the same. In Jesus' name we pray this.

22
OBEDIENCE

Obedience of God's Word is the inevitable fruit of a relationship with Jesus. The focus of this session is to discuss the necessity of obedience to spiritual victory.

God desires our obedience more than anything else we can offer Him.

But Samuel replied, "What is more pleasing to the Lord: your burnt offerings and sacrifices or your obedience to His voice? Listen! Obedience is better than sacrifice, and submission is better than offering the fat of rams." 1 Samuel 15:22

We could do a thousand things for God, but the one thing that He desires most is that we are doing it with a pure heart. God wants our *hearts*. If He can get those, He knows obedience will follow. That is why Proverbs 4:23 says, "Guard your heart above all else, for it determines the course of your life." The heart charts our path. We can give God our money, possessions, service, church attendance, and other sacrifices, but they're valueless without giving Him our heart-led obedience. Do you view obedience as a religion-driven obligation or a relationship-inspired desire?

Love for God results in obedience of His commands and companionship with His Holy Spirit.

[Jesus said,] "If you love Me, obey My commandments. And I will ask the Father, and He will give you another Advocate, who will never leave you. He is the Holy Spirit, who leads into all truth. The world cannot receive Him, because it isn't looking for Him and doesn't recognize Him. But you know Him, because He lives with you now and later will be in you." John 14:15-17

The result of authentic love for God is a life that reflects His Word, and this is a privilege. As 2 Corinthians 5:14 says, "Christ's love controls us." Jesus' love makes us *want* to follow Him. And He gives us the passion to obey through the power of the Holy Spirit—our Helper, our Partner—so that we are directed and protected in every situation. Who has an example of how the Holy Spirit has "[led you] into truth"? Why is it impossible for the world to "recognize" and "receive" the Holy Spirit?

God both impassions us and empowers us for obedience.

For God is working in you, giving you the desire and the power to do what pleases Him. Philippians 2:13

Obedience of God's commands is an unbearable burden—an impossibility—if we do not recognize that only *God* can motivate us and empower us for the assignment He gives. But obedience is a *pleasure* when we are welcoming the Holy Spirit to give us supernatural "desire" and "power." Second Peter 1:3 reminds us, "By [God's] divine power, [He] has given us everything we need for living a godly life." Are we asking God's Holy Spirit daily to first give us the spark to fire us up and second, the fuel to keep the fire lit each day to obey Him?

Obedience brings good things from God.

...[God] will withhold no good thing from those who do what is right. Psalm 84:11

Righteousness and blessings accompany one another all throughout Scripture. God's nature is to reward obedience. When we live according to His Word, He pours out His blessings on us. Far beyond material things, what has God blessed you with during seasons of obedience? Relationships? Wisdom? Peace? Direction? Discernment?

Obedience is motivated by God's redemption and assures God's provision.

"Come now, let's settle this," says the Lord. "Though your sins are like scarlet, I will make them as white as snow. Though they are red like crimson, I will make them as white as wool. If you will only obey Me, you will have plenty to eat." **Isaiah 1:18-19**

Jesus died not only so that we can be saved, but so that we can be sanctified. The blood of Jesus dissolves our greatest sin like scorching hot pavement evaporates a raindrop. The *instant* we repent of our impurity, it's gone. Then the sanctification process begins. How does meditating on Jesus' crucifixion and visualizing His bloody, ravaged body purify our motives for obedience? Doesn't this multiply our gratitude?

Obedience of God's commands connects us to Jesus' presence.

[Jesus said,] "Those who accept My commandments and obey them are the ones who love Me. And because they love Me, My Father will love them. And I will love them and reveal Myself to each of them." **John 14:21**

Disobedience keeps us from experiencing Jesus' presence. Are we in the habit of confessing sin and correcting disobedience so that Jesus "reveals [Himself]" to us?

Once we have received God's grace, we must then reflect God's truth.

Well then, should we keep on sinning so that God can show us more and more of His wonderful grace? Of course not! Since we have died to sin, how can we continue to live in it? **Romans 6:1-2**

Faith saves us, not obedience. But obedience deepens our relationship with God. If we truly grasp the greatness of God's grace, we will fully align our lives with God's truth. Paul makes it clear—we must not abuse God's grace (salvation) by being lazy about our sanctification. How does our obedience show gratefulness for God's sacrifice?

Obedience is the key to spiritual victory.

Loving God means keeping His commandments, and His commandments are not burdensome. For every child of God defeats this evil world, and we achieve this victory through our faith [in Jesus, the Son of God]. **1 John 5:3-5**

Obedience is a blessing, not a burden. It is also a shield. When we obey God's Word, it protects our families and our future. Living within the parameters defined by God's Word brings victory. God's commands set boundaries that limit our flesh but liven our spirit. While boundaries *restrict* our sinful nature, they *free* our nature in Christ. Boundaries ultimately protect blessings. Like a puppy inside a fence, a train on its tracks, or a toddler in his crib, God's Word provides protection and abundance. How has staying within God's boundaries brought *freedom*, not restriction, in your life?

God, obedience is exhausting without Your supernatural sustenance, which is why we desperately need encounters with Your Son and empowerment from Your Spirit. Grant us both the desire and power to follow Your lead in everything we do. In Jesus' name we pray this.

23
WORDS

Our words define the world around us. The focus of this session is to discuss what the Word says about using our tongues to represent Jesus and build God's Kingdom.

Our words bring identity to our lives and the lives of those around us.

The tongue can bring death or life; those who love to talk will reap the consequences. **Proverbs 18:21**

The tongue is a powerful force. It is a tool that establishes identity—a mechanism that can both build and bring life or destroy and bring death. We determine its function by breathing words that are constructive or destructive. God wants to use a warrior's tongue to bring life. Who has an example of how someone else's positive or negative words stuck with you and had a profound impact on what you believed about your identity?

Our words reflect our hearts.

A good person produces good things from the treasury of a good heart, and an evil person produces evil things from the treasury of an evil heart. What you say flows from what is in your heart. **Luke 6:45**

There is a term in computer science that says, "Garbage in, garbage out." This phrase is also spiritually relevant. If our hearts have junk in them, our mouths will spew junk out of them. Honestly, do people associate your words with joy and positivity or discouragement and negativity? What does this indicate about your heart?

We guide our lives by guarding our words.

...For if we could control our tongues, we would be perfect and could also control ourselves in every other way. We can make a large horse go wherever we want by means of a small bit in its mouth. And a small rudder makes a huge ship turn wherever the pilot chooses to go, even though the winds are strong. **James 3:2-4**

Taming the tongue is a momentous task because the urge to speak is often uncontrollable. The compulsion to "let them know how we feel" is tough to restrain in blood-boiling moments. James—Jesus' blood brother and the author of this passage—probably watched Jesus remain gentle (or even silent) on many occasions when situations merited frustration. It is impossible to tame the tongue on our own, but with the Holy Spirit's power, we can speak words that edify. What person in your life is most disciplined when it comes to subduing the impulse to speak harshly?

Warriors tell the truth about everything.

The Lord detests lying lips, but...delights in those who tell the truth. **Proverbs 12:22**

Honesty is the foundation of every relationship. When that foundation cracks, it is usually expensive and messy to repair. This is precisely why God loves truth and hates lies while the enemy loves lies and hates truth. Has a lie ever compromised a relationship in your life?

We defeat feelings of doubt with words of faith.

But Job replied, "...Should we accept only good things from the hand of God and never anything bad?" So in all this, Job said nothing wrong. **Job 2:10**

Job lost literally everything he had as his trust and obedience were tested by God. God eventually restored twice as much back to Job because he resiliently obeyed and *voiced* his faith in God, refusing to let his feelings produce negative words. Psalm 17:3 says we must be "determined not to sin in what [we] say." How does *speaking trust* and rejecting doubt-filled emotions show God that we are serious about our faith?

The fewer the words, the fewer the problems.

Watch your tongue and keep your mouth shut, and you will stay out of trouble. **Proverbs 21:23**

Warriors err on the side of saying less because the higher the word count, the higher the probability we will say something out of God's will. Proverbs 10:19 even says, "Too much talk leads to sin. Be sensible and keep your mouth shut." During your most maddening moments, what helps *you* keep your mouth shut?

We respect confidentiality and only speak uplifting words about others.

A gossip goes around telling secrets, but those who are trustworthy can keep a confidence. **Proverbs 11:13**

People who constantly disparage and discredit others are usually speaking from a place of insecurity or envy. How does comparison steal our joy and cause us to speak condescendingly of others as our defense mechanism?

Our words are always wholesome and encouraging.

Don't use foul or abusive language. Let everything you say be good and helpful, so that your words will be an encouragement to those who hear them. **Ephesians 4:29**

We as men love to tell a good story, get a good laugh, and give a good jab when we're around our buddies. The problem is that anytime our words become unwholesome or are used to slander someone, God's out. Have you ever had a group of friends that seemed to always bash others or initiate immoral jokes and conversations? Did their conversation culture influence you to do the same?

We must let God frequently filter our hearts and our mouths.

May the words of my mouth and the meditation of my heart be pleasing to You, O Lord, my rock and my redeemer. **Psalm 19:14**

Our words have massive impact on what people believe about themselves. Our spouses and children tend to live according to the identity we speak into them. What words can we speak over our spouses and children that "please" God and reinforce *His* identity for their lives?

God, we recognize that not a single word disappears after it is said and that each one shapes the identity of people and circumstances. Cleanse our hearts and mouths of any evil and let Your Spirit guide our tongues to bring life and light to our world. In Jesus' name we pray this.

24
FAITH

Faith is unrelenting belief in God's realness and trust in God's Word. The focus of this session is to discuss what mature faith looks like in a warrior for Jesus.

Jesus is the supernatural substance of faith.

So faith comes from hearing...hearing the Good News about Christ. **Romans 10:17**

The simplest definition of faith is this: trusting and acting in confidence like Jesus is real. And Hebrews 11:6 reminds us that without this confidence, it is *impossible* to please God. Jesus isn't a mascot for a religion or some figurehead for a ritualistic institution. No...He is God. He is Man. He is King. He is Life. He lived a perfect life and died a brutal death, only to embarrass darkness and the grave. And since He did this on the ground we walk on today, it changes *everything*...because no one in history has ever done anything remotely close to this. Can our faith be contagious if we are not truly convinced of the reality of Jesus' existence, life, death, and resurrection?

God can do whatever He wants to do whenever He wants to do it.

Jesus looked at them intently and said, "Humanly speaking, it is impossible. But with God everything is possible." **Matthew 19:26**

Jeremiah 32:17 says, "O Sovereign Lord! You made the heavens and earth by Your strong hand and powerful arm. Nothing is too hard for You!" Faith is knowing that nothing is too difficult for God. If He can split a sea, stop a storm, and bring dead bones to life, He surely can handle anything we face. And *even if* He never performs a miracle in our situation, we must realize that our salvation is the greatest miracle of all. What are you believing for God to do right now that seems stupid on paper but is well within His abilities?

Faith is *certainty* that, even on our worst day, God's plan is better than ours.

And we know that God causes everything to work together for the good of those who love God and are called according to His purpose for them. **Romans 8:28**

God is sovereign. He *is* supreme power. We don't know better than Him. Our perspective is absurdly limited. God's perspective is perplexingly unlimited. No matter what we are facing today, *if* we stay planted in the soil of God's Word, one day we *will* meet that moment when we can say, "God worked this out for my good because He saw a bigger picture all along." It's God's guarantee. Have you ever been discouraged for a season, only to discover later that God was watching out for you?

Faith works while it waits.

Wait patiently for the Lord. Be brave and courageous. Yes, wait patiently for the Lord. **Psalm 27:14**

Waiting on God does not mean being idle. While we wait, we courageously and proactively work on all that *we* can do while God moves. How do prayer and worship simultaneously create supernatural *movement* and *rest?*

Faith translates to immovable obedience.

[Jesus said,] "Remain in Me, and I will remain in you. For a branch cannot produce fruit if it is severed from the vine, and you cannot be fruitful unless you remain in Me." **John 15:4**

Faith *rests* in obedience because obedience nourishes our relationship with God. The greatest evidence of trust during a dry season is *remaining* within God's directives for living life. By doing so, we "let our roots grow down into Him," as Colossians 2:7 says. When we see no movement in our circumstances, we fix our eyes not on what seems stagnant in the seen but on what we are certain is progressing in the unseen, as 2 Corinthians 4:18 tells us to do. When we do this, God produces fruit in us and feeds others through us. How can we leverage the tough seasons to be fruitful seasons?

Our faith in God's follow-through is unbreakable and unwavering.

Abraham never wavered in believing God's promise. In fact, his faith grew stronger, and in this he brought glory to God. He was fully convinced that God is able to do whatever He promises. **Romans 4:20-21**

Abraham and Sarah waited over two *decades* (not weeks, or days, or even years) for the promise of their son, Isaac, to be fulfilled. And Sarah was 90 years old when God's promise finally came to fruition. Ninety. Not 19. God's delay was not denial, but discipline. Abraham, like many of us, needed to be starved of self-reliance and recognize that forcing God's plans outside of His timing complicates everything. God's wisdom is the infrastructure of God's timing. His timing is perfect. Is your faith wavering right now in any situation because it seems like God has not moved in days, weeks, years, or even decades? Is it causing you to wander away or remain rooted?

No matter what we are planning, God's purpose is unfolding.

You can make many plans, but the Lord's purpose will prevail. **Proverbs 19:21**

We cannot stop God's purpose from panning out. His sovereignty is the gatekeeping mechanism for what is and isn't allowed to enter our lives. Making wise, God-honoring choices definitely matters, but God will ultimately use both good and bad outcomes for His purpose. This means we can *relax* about our past and future decision-making as long as we are seeking to honor Him in the present. If God gives us peace about multiple choices regarding a big decision, should we ever be anxious about choosing the "correct" one? Or should we rest in His "prevailing purpose" and simply honor Him with the choice we make?

Faith is in who we know, not what we see.

For we live by believing and not by seeing. **2 Corinthians 5:7**

As Hebrews 11:1 says, "Faith shows the reality of what we hope for; it is the evidence of things we cannot see." Seeing does not lead us to believing. Believing leads us to seeing. It is a relationship with Jesus that allows us to see Him with our mind's eye and see evidence of His existence with our physical eyes. What is some "evidence" you have seen in the natural that came from faith in the supernatural?

God, You are real. We acknowledge right now that You can do anything. We trust Your purpose and Your timing, and we ask that our relationship with You grows deeper and as a result, our faith in You grows stronger. In Jesus' name we pray this.

25
ETERNITY

A warrior sets his sights on eternity, not earth. The focus of this session is to discuss what the Word says about the perfect permanent reality for those who know Jesus.

Whether or not we know Jesus determines our eternity.

For we must all stand before Christ to be judged. We will each receive whatever we deserve for the good or evil we have done in this earthly body. **2 Corinthians 5:10**

Death isn't the most pleasant topic to discuss, but it is inevitable. One out of every one person dies. Then what? The Bible tells us that we will stand before God to be judged. Romans 14:12 says we will "give [our] personal account to God" on how we lived our lives. At that moment, only one thing will matter: Did we know Jesus and live according to God's Word? This consequential answer will determine whether we go to a perfect place called heaven to enjoy God's presence forever or an awful place called hell forever separated from His presence—a reality for those who do not have a relationship with Jesus. If you died right now and faced God, the Father, would your narrative honestly be more about magnifying His Son or satisfying yourself?

Heaven is a perfect place where those who know Jesus will enjoy eternity in God's presence.

[Jesus said,] "I tell you the truth, those who listen to my message and believe in God who sent me have eternal life..." **John 5:24**

The book of Revelation is subject to different views and interpretations about the events to come and eternity. But as we interpret it, if our last breath on earth were today, we will go straight to heaven to be with Jesus as long as we know Him and lived according to His Word. Then we will return with Jesus at His Second Coming and serve Him during His 1,000-year reign here on earth—the time when Satan is "bound" from "deceiving the nations" (Revelation 20). Lastly, God's Final Judgment on the entire universe will commence and we as Jesus' warriors will accompany God to our eternal destination in heaven where we will reside with Jesus forever. Do you know beyond a shadow of a doubt that if you died today, you would be in heaven?

Hell is a horrific place where everything unholy must face God's justice.

...[God] will come with His mighty angels, in flaming fire, bringing judgment on those who don't know [Him] and on those who refuse to obey the Good News of our Lord Jesus. They will be punished with eternal destruction, forever separated from the Lord and from His glorious power. **2 Thessalonians 1:7-9**

God is holy. And because holiness demands justice, everything that is not made holy by the blood of Jesus must face the painful consequences of God's justice. The place where this happens is called hell, and we see all throughout Scripture that being "forever separated" from God yields terrible repercussions—nonstop, eternal fire; torturous suffering; unending pain; and an absence of joy, hope, or second chances. But God is also *love*. Second Peter 3:9 says, "He does not want anyone to be destroyed, but wants everyone to repent." God's character doesn't cast us to hell; *our sin* does. Why must our mission of sharing God's truth with others be taken very seriously?

Heaven is Jesus' home and it is luxury redefined.

[Jesus said,] "There is more than enough room in My Father's home. If this were not so, would I have told you that I am going to prepare a place for you? When everything is ready, I will come and get you, so that you will always be with Me where I am." **John 14:2-3**

The first thing we do when we choose a vacation spot is research it. We want to see pictures and get details and reviews from reputable sources. Those descriptions and visuals are what inspire us to visit a certain place. Shouldn't we do the same research for our final destination? Otherwise, how could we picture it? Heaven is a real space. Revelation 21-22 describes it. Cube-shaped, heaven's "length and width and height [are] each 1,400 miles" with walls "216 feet thick" made of jasper, sapphire, emerald, and other precious stones. The city is "pure gold" but "as clear as glass" with gates made of single pearls, and "the city has no need of sun or moon, for the glory of God illuminates the city, and the Lamb is its light." But there's more: "A river with the water of life, clear as crystal, [flows] from the throne of God and the Lamb," and "nothing evil will be allowed to enter [into the city]...only those whose names are written in the Lamb's Book of Life." Men, heaven is going to be another level. Paradise. Better than Bora Bora...the kind of luxurious destination we can't afford. Yet, it's what awaits us *for eternity* if we invest our lives for Jesus now. What prevents us from getting genuinely fired up about heaven? Is it misinformation or unbelief?

Heaven is a huge, diverse worship party.

After this [John] saw a vast crowd, too great to count, from every nation and tribe and people and language, standing in front of the throne and before the Lamb...And they were shouting with a great roar, "Salvation comes from our God who sits on the throne and from the Lamb!" **Revelation 7:9-10**

When John received his revelation from God, the most rewarding aspect of heaven was this: "God Himself will be with [us]," as Revelation 21:3 says. The Great I Am *and* Jesus Himself will reside with us in this city. Incredible. We will have an all-access pass to an unending worship party with a "vast crowd...from every nation and tribe and people and language." And 1 Thessalonians 4:17 says we will enjoy this electric, unified, loving atmosphere with those we know, each of us with perfected bodies, as 1 Corinthians 15:35-54 tells us. Revelation 21:4 sweetens this reality, revealing that there will be "no more death or sorrow or crying or pain." So, why in the world would we *not* be excited about this dynamic, flawless setting with our Creator?

Warriors live with our home in mind.

Above all, you must live as citizens of heaven, conducting yourselves in a manner worthy of the Good News about Christ... **Philippians 1:27**

What we believe about eternity determines how we live today. We live now for later. There is peace in maintaining shallow roots here on earth. It's why getting rid of piles of pointless stuff and keeping our homes organized and in order brings indescribable peace and freedom. It is in our DNA to long for less because we are not in our permanent homes. We are on a business trip that will end soon. How does *passion* for heaven manifest itself in *preparing* and *planning* for heaven?

God, we cannot wait for the pristine perfection of heaven. Being forever in Your presence will be the best part. Let our aim be on the *realities* of heaven as we live our lives here on earth. In Jesus' name we pray this.

26
FREEDOM

Freedom is found in Jesus—the living Word of God. The focus of this session is to discuss the importance of getting free from sin and staying free as warriors for Jesus.

God purchased our freedom with His Son.

*For [Jesus] has rescued us from the kingdom of darkness and transferred us into the Kingdom of His dear Son, who purchased our freedom and forgave our sins. **Colossians 1:13-14***

Without the shedding of Jesus' blood, we have no freedom, hope, or salvation. It was this sacrifice that sealed and certified our ability to spend eternity with God. Jesus' blood is the red carpet to freedom. After we receive Jesus, the most intimidating thing we can ever face as humans—death—only brings us greater life. Mind-blowing. Should we fear death if it is going to bring ultimate freedom?

Jesus' sacrifice gives freedom to *anyone* who accepts it.

*...There is one God and one Mediator who can reconcile God and humanity—the Man Christ Jesus. He gave His life to purchase freedom for everyone. This is the message God gave to the world at just the right time. **1 Timothy 2:5-6***

There are no qualifiers to receiving the forgiveness and freedom that comes from Jesus. Jesus' blood covers all sin and is available to anyone. Jesus is our Mediator—our Bridge—to God. Who are you praying for right now to be freed by Jesus Christ?

Only Jesus can set us free.

*[Jesus said,] "So if the Son sets you free, you are truly free." **John 8:36***

The only access to true freedom is through Jesus. No self-help, self-discipline, meditation, medication, or good deeds can substitute the decision to make Jesus our Lord and Savior. But even after we receive Jesus, the world will be quick to bring up our past and say that we are not *really* free...that we are not *actually* different after deciding to follow Jesus. Jesus Himself says otherwise. He says we are "truly free" when He sets us free. We are no longer in bondage to sin's penalty or sin's power. Has anyone ever lied to you and brought up your past as the reason why you'll never be different in the future?

God frees us from our past and gives us a new beginning.

*For I am about to do something new. See, I have already begun! Do you not see it? I will make a pathway through the wilderness. I will create rivers in the dry wasteland. **Isaiah 43:19***

No matter who we are or what we have done in our past, God gives us a brand new start when we accept Jesus' forgiveness. When we follow Him, He "create[s] rivers in the dry wasteland." What "pathways" and "rivers" has God provided for you since beginning your life in Christ?

Only the Holy Spirit can keep us free.

So Christ has truly set us free. Now make sure that you stay free, and don't get tied up again in slavery to the law...So I say, let the Holy Spirit guide your lives. Then you won't be doing what your sinful nature craves. **Galatians 5:1,16**

Once we are set free from sin (salvation), we receive the Holy Spirit to help us remain free from sin (sanctification). No one but the Holy Spirit can give us the power to remain free from sin, and Ephesians 5:18 reveals the key to doing this: "be filled with the Holy Spirit." Who can attest to the benefits of the Holy Spirit's partnership?

Sin opposes freedom.

Now may the God of peace make you holy in every way, and may your whole spirit and soul and body be kept blameless until our Lord Jesus Christ comes again. **1 Thessalonians 5:23**

Freedom and holiness are two peas in a pod because they are both set apart from sin. Are there any relationships (or environments) in our lives that seem to always pull us into sin and compete with our freedom?

Forgiving others frees us from the enemy's deception.

...And when I forgive whatever needs to be forgiven, I do so with Christ's authority for your benefit, so that Satan will not outsmart us... **2 Corinthians 2:10-11**

Satan uses unforgiveness to strip away our freedom. By attempting to hold someone else captive for their mistakes, we end up holding ourselves captive. Are we holding any grudges that are giving the enemy license to "outsmart us"?

Satan hates our freedom and wants to keep us in captivity.

[Jesus said,] "The thief's purpose is to steal and kill and destroy. My purpose is to give them a rich and satisfying life." **John 10:10**

As the noted saying goes, "Satan will take us farther than we want to go, keep us longer than we want to stay, and costs us more than we want to pay." The enemy wants to "destroy" every good thing in our lives and keep us shackled to our sinful nature. God, on the other hand, wants us to live a "rich and satisfying life" by freeing us from our sinful nature. How does our role as gatekeepers of our homes protect the freedom of our families? How does prayerfully moderating the media, friends, and influences that enter our homes preserve the most satisfying lives for our families?

Our freedom is not about us; it is about others.

...You have been called to live in freedom...But don't use your freedom to satisfy your sinful nature. Instead, use your freedom to serve one another in love. **Galatians 5:13**

God does not set us free to satisfy our own desires but to serve others and "fish for people," as Matthew 4:19 says. We love others by serving and sharing. Why is it crucial for us to remain free to stay passionate about helping set others free?

God, we honor the sacrifice of Your precious Son. We don't know how You did it, but we thank You for the freedom You purchased with His blood. Let us live in Your Truth as it sets us free and gives us victory. In Jesus' name we pray this.

27

DISCIPLINE

A warrior for Jesus does not exist without discipline. The focus of this session is to discuss the role that discipline plays in being the men God has called us to be.

Discipline is *doing* what we know we need to do.

Now that you know these things, God will bless you for doing them. **John 13:17**

Comfort, convenience, and control are default preferences for humans. We naturally cater to maximizing ease and minimizing energy expenditure. It's the reason why talking the talk is easier than walking the walk. After Jesus washed His disciples' feet and taught them about serving others, He made a simple statement relevant to almost any spiritual principle—*do* what you know you're supposed to do. *Apply* your knowledge. Wisdom is the *application* of God's Word. What we *do*, not what we say, indicates what we believe. What is something you have been talking about needing to do but haven't had the discipline to actually do?

Self-discipline is the highest accomplishment of a human.

Better to be patient than powerful; better to have self-control than to conquer a city. **Proverbs 16:32**

No matter what we achieve professionally, financially, relationally, or even spiritually, those "notches on our belt" are no rival for the achievement of having control over our own bodies. Self-control can be applied to our emotions, thoughts, words, sexual purity, diet and exercise patterns, money management, time management, and even our rest habits. In what area do you know you need more discipline? And how important is accountability in achieving that discipline?

A disciple of Jesus is disciplined at dying to self.

My old self has been crucified with Christ. It is no longer I who live, but Christ lives in me. So I live in this earthly body by trusting in the Son of God, who loved me and gave Himself for me. **Galatians 2:20**

When we decide to follow Jesus, we are not just improved beings. We are *new* beings. At that moment, we put to death our fleshly appetites and immediately become self-deniers so that only Jesus and His desires are living in us. Discipline is painful for our flesh but equals freedom for our spirit. What appetites are the toughest to deny?

We discipline our children the way God disciplines us.

Fathers, do not provoke your children to anger by the way you treat them. Rather, bring them up with the discipline and instruction that comes from the Lord. **Ephesians 6:4**

Deciphering our role as fathers can be difficult when it comes to disciplining our children, but it helps to look through the lens of how our Heavenly Father disciplines us. Romans 2:4 highlights God's gentle disciplinary approach: "Don't you see how wonderfully kind, tolerant, and patient God is with you? ...Can't you see that His *kindness* is intended to turn you from your sin?" God is slow to anger and isn't looking for opportunities to drop a sledgehammer on us. Instead, He draws us to obedience with His kindness. How does connection to the Holy Spirit help us mirror this same disciplinary approach even with rebellious children?

A father's discipline is rooted in love.

[God said,] "For the Lord disciplines those He loves, and He punishes each one He accepts as His child." As you endure this divine discipline, remember that God is treating you as His own children. Who ever heard of a child who is never disciplined by its father? If God doesn't discipline you as He does all of His children, it means that you are illegitimate and are not really His children at all. **Hebrews 12:6-8**

If your 3-year-old son was in the road about to get hit by an 18-wheeler barreling down your street, which of these two responses would indicate genuine love for him—smiling and waving at him, or running full speed and tackling him out of the way of the oncoming semi? Of course the second option would indicate love. God's discipline is similar. It may sting a little when He closes a door to a job, prevents a relationship from working out, or delays giving us the baby we are praying for, but we must trust that He is protecting us from something destructive and saving us for His best. Would you agree that God's discipline is actually a *blessing* that reinforces the value of staying obedient to His instruction?

Warriors practice the discipline of quieting the noise and listening to God.

"Be still, and know that I am God!..." **Psalm 46:10**

We live in a chaotic culture with nonstop noise. How often do we turn off the distractions, read God's Word, and simply listen to what He is trying to tell us? Why is it important for our spouses and children to see us doing this?

Physical and spiritual disciplines are correlated.

I discipline my body like an athlete, training it to do what it should. Otherwise, I fear that after preaching to others I myself might be disqualified. **1 Corinthians 9:27**

A warrior's body is under the absolute authority of Jesus. Our spirit tells our flesh what to do, not the opposite. Our bodies are servants of the Holy Spirit. And we "work hard to show the results of [our] salvation," as Philippians 2:12 says. This ongoing process called sanctification *depends* on discipline. How does being disciplined in our physical health benefit our spiritual health and vice versa?

Discipline demands persistence and perseverance.

[Jesus said,] "Keep on asking, and you will receive what you ask for. Keep on seeking, and you will find. Keep on knocking, and the door will be opened to you." **Luke 11:9**

Spiritual success requires pace and endurance in our prayer life. Do we "keep on asking" when we haven't received an answer to our prayers? Or even tougher, do we "keep on seeking" a deeper relationship with God even after we have received what we have asked for?

God, we know discipline is painful in the present but that it brings a peaceful harvest in the future. Let Your Holy Spirit give us this perspective as we live self-controlled lives that are dead to sin and alive in You. In Jesus' name we pray this.

28
FIGHT

We must fight for spiritual victory. The focus of this session is to discuss what the Word says about the necessity of fighting against the enemy and fighting for Jesus.

We have a legitimate spiritual enemy who must be studied.

[Satan] was a murderer from the beginning. He has always hated the truth, because there is no truth in him. When he lies, it is consistent with his character; for he is a liar and the father of lies. **John 8:44**

We are in a brutal spiritual war with a dangerous opponent—Satan—a former fallen angel named Lucifer who was banished from heaven because of his pride. Men, we must understand that he is shrewd, versatile, adaptable, stealthy, strategic, opportunistic, intelligent, powerful, and persuasive. His strategy is deception and his weapon is lies. He has power greater than ours, and 2 Corinthians 4:4 tells us that he "blinds minds" to keep us from experiencing peace. What are some lies that we hear from the enemy that blind us from reality and prevent us from living in victory?

Satan's power is pathetic, even laughable compared to God's.

"Yes," [Jesus] told them, "I saw Satan fall from heaven like lightning!" **Luke 10:18**

When Satan tried to oppose God—the impressive creation pridefully challenging the immortal Creator—God "reduced [him] to ashes" in a split second, giving us unfair, unrivaled, lopsided authority in spiritual battle. Isaiah 54:17 reminds us that no weapon turned against us will succeed! How does it make you feel to know that you've been granted supernatural authority that ensures victory in spiritual battle?

We dominate in spiritual battle when we operate in our God-given authority.

Look, I have given you authority over all the power of the enemy, and you can walk among snakes and scorpions and crush them. Nothing will injure you. **Luke 10:19**

Our enemy is strong, but Jesus is far stronger. With Jesus in us, we have *complete* dominion and authority over Satan's attacks. Name some of the "power[s] of the enemy" that can we "crush" with Jesus' power.

We must fight to *know God* and *obey God* daily to protect our families.

"...Don't be afraid of the enemy! Remember the Lord, who is great and glorious, and fight for your brothers, your sons, your daughters, your wives, and your homes!" **Nehemiah 4:14**

We face a twofold challenge each day—to know God and obey God. If we want to obey God, we must get to *know* God, because obedience is exhausting without a desire to obey. Spending time with God creates that desire. Are we daily fighting against worldly comforts—like our cozy bed in the mornings—to worship God and read His Word so that we are empowered for obedience? Can this discipline be improved? And from a domestic standpoint, how does working hard to provide financial support for our families (if we are physically and mentally capable) show that we "care for [our] relatives, especially those in [our] own household," as 1 Timothy 5:8 directs us to do?

To "fight for Jesus" in spiritual battle means to maintain a resolute focus on Him, not ourselves, and heaven, not earth.

But you...are a man of God; so run from all these evil things. Pursue righteousness and a godly life, along with faith, love, perseverance, and gentleness. Fight the good fight for the true faith. Hold tightly to the eternal life to which God has called you, which you have declared so well before many witnesses. **1 Timothy 6:11-12**

We are men of God. We are fighters. We are warriors. What earthly things or impure habits typically distract us from fighting for what matters?

When *we* fight to align ourselves with God, *He* fights and wins our battles.

[Jahaziel] said, "Listen, all you people...This is what the Lord says: Do not be afraid! Don't be discouraged by this mighty army, for the battle is not yours, but God's." **2 Chronicles 20:15**

What "mighty" challenges "discourage" us when we try and fight them on our own?

Our spiritual enemy camouflages himself as something appealing to deliver something destructive. Enticement is his undercover entry point for evil.

...Even Satan disguises himself as an angel of light. **2 Corinthians 11:14**

Ezekiel 28 tells us Lucifer was the "model of perfection" and "full of beauty." What are some ways the enemy draws us to something dangerous by using something attractive? How does he use pleasure and comfort to nurture spiritual apathy?

The exact same power that propelled Jesus from the grave is accessible to us through the Holy Spirit.

The Spirit of God, who raised Jesus from the dead, lives in you. And just as God raised Christ Jesus from the dead, He will give life to your mortal bodies by this same Spirit living within you. **Romans 8:11**

It is mind-blowing that we can receive the identical source of power in our veins that fueled Jesus' miracles on earth. How often do we reflect on just how dynamic the power of God must be to literally annihilate death's entire identity?

Encounters with Jesus equip us for spiritual victory.

As [Saul] was approaching Damascus on this mission, a light from heaven suddenly shone down around him. He fell to the ground... **Acts 9:3-4**

Saul in the New Testament was known for his brutality toward Christians. Acts 9:1 says he "was eager to kill the Lord's followers." But on his way to Damascus to carry out this horrific mission, Saul had an *encounter* with Jesus that singlehandedly transformed his life. The rest is history—Saul, also known as Paul the Apostle, went on to be filled with the Spirit and wrote some of the most powerful books of the New Testament. How can one moment in close proximity of Jesus totally transform us?

God, we recognize that we are in a spiritual war against a legitimate opponent, but we also know that with Your presence, nothing can destroy or defeat us. Let us encounter Jesus and arm ourselves daily with the Word and Your Holy Spirit to keep us living in victory. In Jesus' name we pray this.

29
IDENTITY

Our identity is defined by who God says we are. The focus of this session is to discuss how knowing our identity helps us walk confidently as warriors for Jesus.

An identity built on Jesus is sturdy and secure.

For no one can lay any foundation other than the one we already have—Jesus Christ. **1 Corinthians 3:11**

Identity can be misplaced in almost anything—the way we look, the clothes we wear, the money we make, the vehicle we drive, the record we set, the position we hold, the number of followers we have. The list goes on. Whatever we want to be "known" for—our "calling card"—is usually where we misplace identity and draw validation. How does misplacing our identity in worldly things always eventually result in insecurity or rejection? Can we ever do enough today to maintain the world's approval tomorrow?

Our style may change, but our standard does not.

So you must remain faithful to what you have been taught from the beginning. If you do, you will remain in fellowship with the Son and with the Father. **1 John 2:24**

Our identity is sturdy and secure in Jesus, but it is also steady. While culture's standards shift by the minute, who we are remains planted in God's Word. The style of our hair and the fit of our jeans may change, but not the standard of our spiritual identity. Have you ever been made fun of for your physical identity? Has anyone ever ridiculed you for your spiritual identity?

We are alive because Jesus is alive.

For the sin of this one man, Adam, caused death to rule over many. But even greater is God's wonderful grace and His gift of righteousness, for all who receive it will live in triumph over sin and death through this one Man, Jesus Christ. Yes, Adam's one sin brings condemnation for everyone, but Christ's one act of righteousness brings a right relationship with God and new life for everyone. Because one person disobeyed God, many became sinners. But because one other Person obeyed God, many will be made righteous. **Romans 5:17-19**

We used to be in the first Adam, but praise God we are now in the second Adam—Jesus Christ. We all once were dead and unrighteous because of our sin, but now we are alive and righteous because of God's grace. How did Jesus' resurrection bring forth unprecedented hope for the world? How do you think modern media outlets would explain away Jesus' resurrection as a hoax if it happened today?

We are spiritual fighters armed with supernatural power and protection.

A final word: Be strong in the Lord and in His mighty power. Put on all of God's armor so that you will be able to stand firm against all strategies of the devil. For we are not fighting against flesh-and-blood enemies, but against evil rulers and authorities of the unseen world, against mighty powers in this dark world, and against evil spirits in the heavenly places. **Ephesians 6:10-12**

Part of our identity is that we are spiritual warriors in a complex war. The war is happening in a supernatural, invisible realm, but it can be impacted by our use of supernatural weapons in the natural realm. In other words, God designed us to fight remotely in the realm we *can* see because it has decisive consequences in the all-important battle happening in a realm we *cannot* see. The effects of this war ultimately manifest themselves right back here in the realm we can see. Why is it important to understand that people in the natural are never the problem, but that evil authorities in the supernatural are the masterminds behind the curtain?

We are victors...*when* we fight.

For the Lord your God is going with you! He will fight for you against your enemies, and He will give you victory! **Deuteronomy 20:4**

Winning is only for the willing. But when we make the decision to step on the battlefield with Jesus, we win. Just how God gave His people victory over their physical enemies in the Old Testament, He promises victory for us today over every spiritual enemy we face—fear, doubt, guilt, shame, temptation, discouragement, depression, addiction. Have you ever seen a lopsided victory in any kind of competition? How is our dominion over evil similar?

Warriors are concerned with internal character, not external appearance.

*But the Lord said to Samuel, "Don't judge by his appearance or height, for I have rejected him. The Lord doesn't see things the way you see them. People judge by outward appearance, but the Lord looks at the heart." **1 Samuel 16:7***

The world's measuring stick is external and predictable. It's all about how impressive your physical stature is, how handsome your face is, how chiseled your physique is, and how spectacular your resume is. God cares about just one metric—how pure your heart is. Have you ever disqualified yourself (or someone else) from God's assignment based off of a flawed metric of the world?

We fear the Lord but never people.

Fearing people is a dangerous trap, but trusting the Lord means safety. **Proverbs 29:25**

Fear of people often translates to our being anxious for their validation. This sprouts from the lie that people have more power than God. We try to please who we fear most. We naturally seek the approval of that which has the greatest authority over us. Psalm 118:6 says, "The Lord is for me, so I will have no fear. What can mere people do to me?" Are there any areas where you still find yourself fearing rejection and needing affirmation from others? How does social media influence our identity measurement standard?

God, we do not base our worth or identity on whether we are decorated or celebrated by society. We declare that our identity is defined by Your Word and that nothing we attain on earth except a relationship with Jesus amounts to anything in the end. Let our allegiance be to pleasing you, not appeasing the world. In Jesus' name we pray this.

30
CONTENTMENT

Contentment is a determination to fixate on God's blessings. The focus of this session is to discuss what the Word says about the fullness of God and the emptiness of the world.

Contentment is inevitable when God establishes His desires as our desires.

Take delight in the Lord, and He will give you your heart's desires. **Psalm 37:4**

This powerful passage reveals the secret to contentment—receiving God's desires in our hearts. Contentment does not happen when God *delivers* our wants but when He *defines* our wants. We misinterpret this verse if we translate it to mean God is a vending machine that dispenses whatever we ask for as long as we please Him. No, God wants to establish *His* wants as our wants—for us to acquire His heart and live for Him. How does God change our desires when we give Him our hearts?

Obsess over Jesus. Everything else is worthless.

But as I looked at everything I had worked so hard to accomplish, it was all so meaningless—like chasing the wind... **Ecclesiastes 2:11**

Solomon—the author of Ecclesiastes and one of the monetarily richest people to ever live on the earth—made this profound statement near the end of his life as he reflected on the purpose of life. Though he had amassed what scholars believe was *trillions* of dollars in wealth, he lamented that all of it was "meaningless." Why is it so challenging for us to acknowledge the reality that worldly things are worthless? Is it because by doing so, we admit most of our pursuits are a waste of time?

Contentment is not dependent upon what we have or don't have.

I know how to live on almost nothing or with everything. I have learned the secret of living in every situation, whether it is with a full stomach or empty, with plenty or little. For I can do everything through Christ, who gives me strength. **Philippians 4:12-13**

As inspirational as it may be to apply this well-known scripture to sports feats, business achievements, or personal aspirations, Paul was actually acknowledging that no matter our situation, as long as we have Jesus, we can be content. This discipline of contentment is not dependent on a number in a bank account, a Range Rover in our garage, or a gourmet meal on the table. Contentment is a focus on the abundance of Jesus and heaven. Why is it a beneficial discipline to reflect on how much *worse* so many others across the world have it?

Contentment finds reasons to be thankful in every situation.

Be thankful in all circumstances, for this is God's will for you... **1 Thessalonians 5:18**

One aspect of discerning God's will is simple—to be thankful...all the time. How often do you tell others around you what you're grateful for? Why is this an invaluable habit for us to practice, especially with our spouses and children?

We must fight against ourselves to maintain a loose grip on worldly things.

Yet true godliness with contentment is itself great wealth. After all, we brought nothing with us when we came into the world, and we can't take anything with us when we leave it. **1 Timothy 6:6-7**

Billy Graham once said, "I never saw a U-Haul behind a hearse." In other words, what we accumulate on earth is ultimately worthless. This is liberating...and great motivation to fight against tightfistedness. What is something far more substantial than possessions and wealth that we can leave behind for others?

We are content not because we have everything we want but because God is everything we need.

Don't love money; be satisfied with what you have. For God has said, "I will never fail you. I will never abandon you." **Hebrews 13:5**

There is nothing accidental about God's provision for His children. He gets to us what He wants to get to us and withholds from us what He wants to withhold from us. He promises this in Deuteronomy 28:12, saying, "[I] will send rain at the proper time from [my] rich treasury in the heavens." We can be sure that the timing and amount of His provision are what He intended them to be. How does comparison destroy contentment and cause us to covet the fortune of others?

Complaint and contentment cannot coexist.

Do everything without complaining and arguing...shining like bright lights in a world full of crooked and perverse people. **Philippians 2:14-15**

Self-pity, complaining, and negativity are from the enemy because they fail to recognize God's goodness. This victimization mentality dwells on lack, not sufficiency. It focuses on being unnoticed, not unworthy. We combat this with resilient gratitude. How is complaining an insult to God's plan?

A warrior loyally reserves his eyes, passion, and affection for his wife.

May your fountain be blessed, and may you rejoice in the wife of your youth. **Proverbs 5:18**

Even if we are not married, we can refuse to settle for anything but God's best by reserving all of our emotional and sexual desires for our wives. God wants His class of warriors to "keep our eyes on our own paper." Our wives are our *only* standard. Every thought, glance, fantasy, emotion, or touch given to *any* woman outside of our wives (before or during marriage) is adopting an unholy standard, and it is stealing transactions intended to be deposited into our wives' value. It is making withdrawals from God's best for intimacy and sex, which is reserved for the confines of a marriage between *one man* and *one woman*. This is God's unchanging standard for us as humans, no matter how much our desires "evolve." How do dating, pursuing, and cherishing our wives add enjoyment to our marriages and keep the fire blazing?

God, it may be depressing for our flesh to admit that the world has nothing to offer us, but it is liberating for our spirit. When we receive Your heart, we receive contentment that rests in the fact that Jesus is alive and that heaven is going to blow our minds. Let us live gratefully aware of these truths. In Jesus' name we pray this.

31
CONFIDENCE

Confidence in Jesus as our identity is crucial for spiritual victory. The focus of this session is to discuss what the Word says about standing confidently as warriors for Jesus.

We are confident that Jesus is beside us and that victory is certain.

Don't be afraid, for I am with you. Don't be discouraged, for I am your God. I will strengthen you and help you. I will hold you up with my victorious right hand. **Isaiah 41:10**

Confidence is brittle and unstable unless it is built on Jesus. Putting confidence in ourselves or others will eventually leave us disappointed, but confidence in Jesus never will. His resurrection validates unshakable confidence. What do you picture when you think of the power of God's "victorious right hand" that crushed the enemy and raised Jesus from the dead?

Warriors are afraid of nothing.

This is my command—be strong and courageous! Do not be afraid or discouraged. For the Lord your God is with you wherever you go. **Joshua 1:9**

Our confidence in Jesus cannot be fazed. Our eternity is certain. Plus, Jesus is our personal security detail for our time on earth, so there is nothing legitimate to fear. This is massive. Because Jesus is with us, the enemy has two choices: get out of the way or get run over. What are some illegitimate fears that we legitimize at times?

We confidently proclaim Jesus every chance we get.

...I am not ashamed of this Good News about Christ. It is the power of God at work, saving everyone who believes—the Jew first and also the Gentile. **Romans 1:16**

Jesus wasn't obnoxious in sharing the Gospel, forcefully bulldozing others with truth, but He absolutely took every opportunity to share. He would firmly voice the truth and then, regardless of the response, He would move on to tell others the great news. Warriors do not shy away from chances to endorse God and testify to His power. We boldly insert Jesus into every conversation because He is *power*. If there was a vaccine that gave every recipient immunity from death, what would we do to get the word out to people? Isn't that exactly what administering the blood of Jesus does?

We are confident that God genuinely loves being involved in our lives.

The Lord directs the steps of the godly. He delights in every detail of their lives. **Psalm 37:23**

When we remain in step with God, He becomes enthralled with even the tiniest aspects of our lives. Like a father on Christmas morning soaking up the details of special moments with his children, God loves immersing Himself in every intricate piece of our lives as we follow the lead of His Word and His Spirit. How does God's interest in the details of our lives instill confidence that God is personable, not distant?

We stand confidently in every circumstance knowing God allowed them.

We can make our plans, but the Lord determines our steps. **Proverbs 16:9**

We are incapable of creating situations that have not been permitted by God. We can *plan*, but in the end, God determines what can and can't happen. Have you ever set an expectation for your plan only to have God let a different one pan out?

Confidence comes from walking in *my* calling, not someone else's.

Pay careful attention to your own work, for then you will get the satisfaction of a job well done, and you won't need to compare yourself to anyone else. **Galatians 6:4**

Comparison kills confidence. Fixating on someone else's assignment blinds us to the truths of Psalm 139:13 and Ephesians 2:10—that each of us from the moment of conception "in [our] mother's womb" becomes a unique "masterpiece" with premeditated purpose. Warriors are confident in our design. Even our perceived flaws were calculated brushstrokes by our Creator to accomplish something specific. What do you believe God designed you to do for His Kingdom?

Jesus stands up for us when we stand confidently for Him.

[Jesus said,] "...Everyone who acknowledges Me publicly here on earth, the Son of Man will also acknowledge in the presence of God's angels..." **Luke 12:8**

In Acts 7:55-56, the Bible's first martyr, Stephen, was stoned to death for standing for Jesus. Jesus then literally stood up for Him! Jesus got up from His seat and showed honor to Stephen for his boldness. What does this say about Jesus' heart—that the King honors us when we refuse to renounce His name?

Jesus understands everything we face because He has already faced it all.

So then, since we have a great High Priest who has entered heaven, Jesus the Son of God, let us hold firmly to what we believe. This High Priest of ours understands our weaknesses, for He faced all of the same testings we do, yet He did not sin. So let us come boldly to the throne of our gracious God. There we will receive His mercy, and we will find grace to help us when we need it most. **Hebrews 4:14-16**

Jesus endured *every* type of pain and temptation so that He would be the ideal High Priest—the perfect Intercessor and Mediator who has felt it all. Isaiah 53:3 says He was "despised...rejected...and acquainted with deepest grief." Why does it bring comfort and confidence when someone else has walked in our shoes?

Our confidence in God's hearing makes miracles possible.

...They rolled [Lazarus'] stone aside. Then Jesus looked up to heaven and said, "Father, thank You for hearing Me. You always hear Me..." **John 11:41-42**

Jesus thanked God for hearing His request even *before* this dead man, Lazarus, came out from the grave. Confidence in God's listening ear preceded a miracle. How does believing that God hears us change the authenticity of our prayers?

God, You are our confidence. Without Your Son, we are nothing. Thank You for being in us, walking with us, fighting for us, and listening to us. Give us confidence to walk in *Your* calling for our lives. In Jesus' name we pray this.

32
JOY

Joy defines the attitude of a warrior. The focus of this session is to discuss what the Word says about the disciplined decisions that cultivate joy.

We are joyful because the Lord is trustworthy.

...We can trust everything [the Lord] does. **Psalm 33:4**

Proverbs 16:20 tells us that "those who trust the Lord will be joyful." If trusting God generates joy, then fear and worry will eliminate joy. We cannot cycle worrisome thoughts through our minds and expect to maintain joy. What triggers tend to incite worry and dampen your joy? Is it your health? Your finances? Your future?

We are joyful because Jesus eliminated the gap between us and God.

And I am convinced that nothing can ever separate us from God's love. Neither death nor life, neither angels nor demons, neither our fears for today nor our worries about tomorrow—not even the powers of hell can separate us from God's love. No power in the sky above or in the earth below—indeed, nothing in all creation will ever be able to separate us from the love of God that is revealed in Christ Jesus our Lord. **Romans 8:38-39**

No mistake we make, fear we face, or force that opposes us can disqualify us from God's love. This is true for one reason and one reason only—Jesus' death. Jesus' blood is the powerful force that neutralizes every opposition and connects us to God's love. Separation from God was eliminated by a crimson bridge. The gap is gone. What in your past needs to be reminded that "the gap is gone"?

We are joyful because God is with us and for us.

[God said,] "When you go through deep waters, I will be with you. When you go through rivers of difficulty, you will not drown. When you walk through the fire of oppression, you will not be burned up; the flames will not consume you." **Isaiah 43:2**

God walks with His warriors through every environment, and He is not intimidated by adverse conditions. Knowing He is right beside us and is unfazed brings peace and joy. As Romans 8:31 reminds us, "If God is for us, who can ever be against us?" The answer is no one. Have you ever experienced unexplainable joy in the midst of a trial or tragedy because you acknowledged the Lord's presence?

Joy is substantial, not circumstantial.

Even though the fig trees have no blossoms, and there are no grapes on the vines; even though the olive crop fails, and the fields lie empty and barren; even though the flocks die in the fields, and the cattle barns are empty, yet I will rejoice in the Lord! I will be joyful in the God of my salvation! **Habakkuk 3:17-18**

Joy is far more than an emotion based on our circumstance or DNA makeup. Joy is a confidence based on substance. Happiness is fickle, but joy is final. When everything appears to be "empty" and "failing," happiness may subside, but joy can remain because it is anchored to the concrete fact that Jesus already won. Some may call it "fake" when we smile and celebrate even when a situation looks grim, but that is what we call leadership. It takes *effort* to choose joy. It is a *discipline* to remember the final score when we feel beat down at halftime. Do you know anyone who is almost annoyingly joyful no matter what is happening around them? Do our families see this kind of maturity in leading our homes?

Joy is the supernatural light in the midst of natural darkness.

Why am I discouraged? Why is my heart so sad? I will put my hope in God! I will praise Him again—my Savior and my God! **Psalm 42:11**

Heaviness and discouragement *will* come, but this passage and Isaiah 61:3 give us the antidote: to praise God. It's simple in theory but difficult to do in seemingly hopeless moments. We defeat depression by drowning it out with praise to our God. Darkness can be a blessing when it draws us to the light because joy emerges from being in close proximity to that light. Joy comes from trusting God even when things don't make a lick of sense. Does anyone have an example of how blaring praise music and worshiping God helped alleviate some heaviness you were carrying?

Joy increases by connecting, discovering, and serving.

Oh, the joys of those who do not follow the advice of the wicked, or stand around with sinners, or join in with mockers. But they delight in the law of the Lord, meditating on it day and night. They are like trees planted along the riverbank, bearing fruit each season. Their leaves never wither, and they prosper in all they do. **Psalm 1:1-3**

Pastor Mark E. Moore, in his book, *Core 52*, offers a profound outlook on joy as it relates to the Word of God. He draws a direct correlation between the three "happy hormones" of our brain—oxytocin (the chemical of comfort), dopamine (the chemical of adventure), and serotonin (the chemical of respect)—and the three specific actions outlined in the three verses above from Psalm 1. It is scientifically proven that this cocktail of chemicals is released when we *connect* to godly relationships (oxytocin - verse 1), *discover* God's Word (dopamine - verse 2), and *serve* those around us (serotonin - verse 3). This revelation that God even wired our brains to experience greater joy based on His biblical mandates is fascinating. Why did God intend for joyfulness to be contingent upon obedience? And doesn't the fact that God gave us His instruction prove that He indeed cares about our happiness?

Adversity purifies our joy.

Dear brothers and sisters, when troubles of any kind come your way, consider it an opportunity for great joy. **James 1:2**

We must recognize that suffering is a gift because it strips away all of the worldly, counterfeit substitutes for joy. We try to avoid anything uncomfortable, but it is discomfort that produces the most abundant joy. Sports, music, money, popularity, entertainment...these are medicinal patches that offer mere emotion. But *pure* joy is when Jesus is *all* we have, when nothing else is contaminating His full presence. When God allows trouble in our lives, how does it exploit the volatility and fragility of the idols we depend on for happiness?

God, if Your Son didn't die for us and defeat death, we would have no hope. But because He did, we always have a reason to be joyful. Let Your Holy Spirit guide us to choose joy no matter what we face. In Jesus' name we pray this.

33
LEADERSHIP

Real leadership points people to the blood of Jesus. The focus of this session is to discuss what biblical leadership looks like.

A real leader is a disciple of Jesus.

If you listen to these commands of the Lord your God...and if you carefully obey them, the Lord will make you the head and not the tail, and you will always be on top and never at the bottom. **Deuteronomy 28:13**

If we asked 100 people to define "leadership," we would probably receive 100 different definitions, but we know that the greatest leader to ever live is Jesus Christ of Nazareth. Therefore, the truest form of leadership is discipleship—becoming like Jesus. The greatest *leader* is the greatest *disciple*. God's promise is that leadership blossoms when we "obey [His] commands." He makes us "the head" and puts us at "the top." What qualities or people do you think of when you hear the term "leader"?

Leaders patiently follow God's lead.

Don't say, "I will get even for this wrong." Wait for the Lord to handle the matter. **Proverbs 20:22**

Leadership looks to God first when challenges arise. We as men are wired to fix problems, but God is the ultimate problem solver. Even if our solution makes the most sense on paper and we can check something off the "to-do list," consulting with God before anything else shows wisdom. When we don't have peace about responding to someone or something, we "wait for the Lord to handle the matter." Why are patience and restraint two essential traits of a leader?

Leaders don't brag on themselves.

When people commend themselves, it doesn't count for much. The important thing is for the Lord to commend them. **2 Corinthians 10:18**

Insecurity tends to mask itself with pride. Pride is a defense mechanism—an overcompensation—for insecurity. When we are starving for validation, we create insulation out of our own praise. Strong leaders don't strive to speak in the spotlight but rather serve in the shadows. How does deflecting praise to others and giving credit to those around us garner God's endorsement?

Leaders do not have favorites.

Then Peter replied, "I see very clearly that God shows no favoritism." **Acts 10:34**

Jesus never excluded based on someone's socioeconomic status, appearance, popularity, genetics, cleanliness, or even their health. He was approachable and inclusive to anyone who desired to be close to Him. Are we always looking to reach every kind of person with the Gospel and help them be discipled? Or do we have our comfortable clique to just enjoy life with?

Leaders honor authority.

Everyone must submit to governing authorities. For all authority comes from God, and those in positions of authority have been placed there by God. **Romans 13:1**

Unless an authority commands us to disobey something in God's Word, we respect their position as God-ordained and we humbly honor their requests. And we as warriors assume a servant's role whether we are running a Fortune 500 company or bagging groceries at the local mart. We honor others because of our testimony, not their title. How do "praying for *all* who are in authority" and "living quiet lives marked by godliness" (as 1 Timothy 2:2 instructs) draw and lead others to Jesus?

Leadership is refined by suffering.

...And it was only right that [God] should make Jesus, through His suffering, a perfect leader, fit to bring [His children] into their salvation. **Hebrews 2:10**

Jesus is the "perfect leader," and we see here that "suffering" qualified Him as such. Has a painful experience ever been a catalyst in developing leadership qualities in you? How does suffering equip us to lead others facing similar trials?

Sin destroys leaders.

When you follow the desires of your sinful nature, the results are very clear: sexual immorality, impurity, lustful pleasures, idolatry, sorcery, hostility, quarreling, jealousy, outbursts of anger, selfish ambition, dissension, division, envy, drunkenness, wild parties, and other sins like these. Let me tell you again, as I have before, that anyone living that sort of life will not inherit the Kingdom of God. **Galatians 5:19-21**

It only takes a glance at the latest news headlines to see that high-profile men fall from leadership daily because of sin. Prominent evangelist from the 1800's Dwight L. Moody once issued this warning to us: "Christians should live in the world, but not be filled with it. A ship lives in the water; but if the water gets into the ship, she goes to the bottom. So Christians may live in the world; but if the world gets into them, they sink." How does surrounding ourselves with other Jesus-focused leaders protect us from "sinking" due to a collision with worldly temptation?

Leaders recognize that their power is *from* God and *for* God.

"Why don't you talk to me?" Pilate demanded. "Don't you realize that I have the power to release you or crucify you?"

Then Jesus said, "You would have no power over Me at all unless it were given to you from above..." **John 19:10-11**

Just before Jesus was sentenced to death, Pilate pridefully claimed that *he* held the power to determine Jesus' fate. Jesus quickly corrected Pilate, reiterating that *God* designates and delegates power as He sees fit. God holds the keys to the leadership kingdom. We are mistaken if we believe that any power we hold was not *granted* to us by God. What are some practical, applicable ways we can point to Jesus with the power God has granted us?

God, Your Son is the leadership prototype. We seek to serve others the way Jesus served others and follow You the way Jesus followed You. Let us use our power to promote and position others for Your glory. In Jesus' name we pray this.

34
GENTLENESS

Gentleness is a trademark of the most Spirit-led warriors. The focus of this session is to discuss what the Word says about the power of gentleness.

The most powerful force in existence is gentle.

"Go out and stand before me on the mountain," the Lord told [Elijah]. And as Elijah stood there, the Lord passed by, and a mighty windstorm hit the mountain. It was such a terrible blast that the rocks were torn loose, but the Lord was not in the wind. After the wind there was an earthquake, but the Lord was not in the earthquake. And after the earthquake there was a fire, but the Lord was not in the fire. And after the fire there was the sound of a gentle whisper. When Elijah heard it, he wrapped his face in his cloak and went out and stood at the entrance of the cave. **1 Kings 19:11-13**

An invaluable lesson for us as husbands, fathers, and leaders is found in this passage. God displays three of His most powerful forces of nature to Elijah—the wind, an earthquake, and a fire—but God revealed the *most* powerful force in the finale, upstaging the others with the *Holy Spirit*. But look at how the Spirit made His presence known: a "gentle whisper" was His method of choice. Hear this, men: The most powerful force in existence—the Holy Spirit—manifests Himself through *gentleness*. He communicates in a whisper. He didn't come in puffed up, chest out, scowl on His face "showing everyone who is in charge." His quiet confidence and tender compassion didn't need loud shouting and aggression to get the point across. Although at times there may need to be strength in rebuking rebellion (as Jesus demonstrated with the Pharisees), warriors default to gentleness. How can we apply this to our role as authorities in our homes? Doesn't this mean our tone should be restrained and relaxed even when we are disrespected by our spouses or children?

The purpose for Jesus' life on earth was driven by grace and gentleness.

God sent His Son into the world not to judge the world, but to save the world through Him. **John 3:17**

The entire purpose of Jesus' assignment from the Father was not one of anger and condemnation but of grace and gentleness. Luke 19:10 tells us that Jesus "came to seek and save those who are lost." Typically, search-and-rescue teams aren't exasperated with the person they are desperate to find. Instead, compassion inspires the persistence of a determined search party. A great litmus test for our gentleness as Christians is this: Does someone else's sin spawn a desire in us for them to experience the *love* of God or the *wrath* of God?

God is gentle, patient, and compassionate.

The Lord is merciful and compassionate, slow to get angry and filled with unfailing love...He showers compassion on all His creation. **Psalm 145:8-9**

Are we *approachable* when someone has wronged us or a child has disobeyed us, or are those around us terrified to face us when they have made a mistake? Which of those two mirrors God as described in this passage?

God prefers kindness as His agent of change.

Don't you see how wonderfully kind, tolerant, and patient God is with you?...Can't you see that His kindness is intended to turn you from your sin? **Romans 2:4**

While the enemy shamefully condemns, Jesus gently convicts us of impurity. God's nature is not to zap us with lightning the moment we make a mistake. He is "wonderfully kind and patient" with us, and His heart is to inspire our u-turn from sin with gentleness, not forcefulness. How can we as fathers firmly stand on truth while gently offering grace when our children stray from obedience? How does *calmly* punishing our children for mistakes and enforcing consequences demonstrate perfect love—the balance of truth and grace?

God is a tenderhearted Father who is drawn to His brokenhearted children.

The Lord is close to the brokenhearted; He rescues those whose spirits are crushed. **Psalm 34:18**

God is acutely aware of our heartbreak and heartache. He promises to be near us in times of brokenness. This is true masculinity. Are we humble enough to express sadness and empathy as husbands and fathers? Do we see vulnerability as a strength or weakness?

Gentleness indicates consideration for others.

Let everyone see that you are considerate in all you do. **Philippians 4:5**

Picture yourself politely showing an elderly lady through a doorway. You are smiling, with one arm holding the door open and the other extended out with an open hand as you patiently usher her over the threshold into another space. This is the picture of consideration. This is the picture of gentleness. Does this kind of considerate, "you first" posture define the tone of our interactions amid conflict?

Holy Spirit-led gentleness restrains anger from becoming sin.

And "don't sin by letting anger control you." Don't let the sun go down while you are still angry, for anger gives a foothold to the devil. **Ephesians 4:26-27**

Gentleness eludes arguments. Proverbs 20:3 says, "Avoiding a fight is a mark of honor." But when disagreements arise, we must realize that it is not a sin to be angry. Anger is inevitable at times. But if we choose to "unleash" our frustration with hurtful words or physical rage, it *becomes* sin and "gives a foothold to the devil," especially when we go to bed angry. We give the enemy permission to infiltrate our marriages and create division and destruction in our homes when we choose to sleep on that resentment. It may be difficult to do after a blood-boiling disagreement, but veteran warriors at least *try* to extend forgiveness even if our spouses reject it. How does speaking scripture even silently to ourselves in the middle of conflict safeguard from "letting anger control [us]"?

God, we are so grateful for Your gentle compassion. You are a mighty God with unmatchable power, yet You are an intimate, approachable, good God. Let us reflect this same considerate, tenderhearted nature to the people around us. In Jesus' name we pray this.

35
FASTING

Fasting is an essential discipline of warriors. The focus of this session is to discuss the importance of disconnecting from the world and connecting to God.

Fasting is about reordering and reinvigorating our relationship with God.

[God said,] "...this is the kind of fasting I want: Free those who are wrongly imprisoned; lighten the burden of those who work for you. Let the oppressed go free, and remove the chains that bind people. Share your food with the hungry, and give shelter to the homeless. Give clothes to those who need them, and do not hide from relatives who need your help. Then your salvation will come like the dawn, and your wounds will quickly heal. Your godliness will lead you forward, and the glory of the Lord will protect you from behind. Then when you call, the Lord will answer. 'Yes, I am here,' He will quickly reply." Isaiah 58:6-9,11

The discipline of fasting is about disconnecting from the world and connecting to God. Fasting quiets the noise to sensitize our ears to the Holy Spirit's voice. As we see in Isaiah 58, when we minimize earthly distractions and eliminate the multitude of idolatrous substitutes that appetize our flesh (like food, drink, sports, shopping, stocks, music, technology, or media), God speaks clearly to us about *His* heart—freeing others from sin. Fasting ultimately reinvigorates our relationship with Jesus and resets our focus on being Gospel spreaders. What habit would be the hardest for us to fast? And why is it beneficial for us to fast what we love most?

Fasting is the spiritual discipline of denying flesh-led appetites to draw closer to God.

For I have told you often before, and I say it again with tears in my eyes, that there are many whose conduct shows they are really enemies of the cross of Christ. They are headed for destruction. Their god is their appetite, they brag about shameful things, and they think only about this life here on earth. But we are citizens of heaven, where the Lord Jesus Christ lives. Philippians 3:18-20

It is effortless to "think only about this life here on earth" and make our "appetite" our "god." But fasting—willfully refraining from feeding *physical* appetites—cultivates a greater desperation for *spiritual* sustenance. As we rid ourselves of worldly dependencies, we find ourselves drawing near to God for nourishment. Emptiness attracts God's presence. Emptiness also matures our discipline to deny ourselves when strength is absent (see Luke 9:23). How does saying "no" to our appetites *during* a fast prepare us to live in obedience on the exhausting days *after* the fast?

Fasting detoxifies my spirit.

Do not stifle the Holy Spirit. 1 Thessalonians 5:19

Warriors take inventory often of worldly things that have embedded into our hearts and habits. Being deliberate about annihilating every toxic impostor that competes with the Holy Spirit is crucial. What specific idols and sins have "stifled" (or suffocated) the Holy Spirit in your life?

Fasting is *not* about a show of suffering for God.

[God said,] "'We have fasted before you!' [My people] say. 'Why aren't you impressed? We have been very hard on ourselves, and You don't even notice it!'

"I will tell you why!" I respond. "It's because you are fasting to please yourselves...This kind of fasting will never get you anywhere with Me. You humble yourselves by going through the motions of penance... Is this what you call fasting? Do you really think this will please the Lord?"' Isaiah 58:3-5

Matthew 6:16-18 reminds us that fasting should never be about gaining attention for ourselves. The passage above from Isaiah echoes the same sentiment. God is speaking to His people—the Israelites—and is clarifying how *not* to fast. God uncovers the self-centered motives of Israel's fasting and how fasting is not about torturously starving ourselves to impress Him or robotically going through the motions of self-punishment to garner the attention of others. Have you ever fasted from something (even just for a meal or for a day)? If so, what was your motive for fasting?

Fasting with the right motives produces intense, effective prayers.

...I gave orders for all of us to fast and humble ourselves before our God. We prayed that He would give us a safe journey and protect us, our children, and our goods as we traveled. So we fasted and earnestly prayed that our God would take care of us, and He heard our prayer. Ezra 8:23

Ezra declared a fast as his people embarked on their journey from Babylon to Jerusalem. Ezra's motivation for fasting was to acknowledge their dependence on God. Notice how Ezra wasn't fasting to lose weight, look better, or get fit. Although these *physical* benefits can certainly manifest in the process, Ezra's motive was *spirtual*. His priority was to glorify God's greatness, as was Daniel's in Daniel 9 as he fasted. Do you have an example of how God has responded in an eye-opening, obvious way to your prayers during a fast?

Fasting brings vision, clarity, and answers.

When this vision came to me, I, Daniel, had been in mourning for three whole weeks. All that time I had eaten no rich food. No meat or wine crossed my lips...until those three weeks had passed...As I was standing on the bank of the great Tigris River, I looked up and saw a man dressed in linen clothing, with a belt of pure gold around his waist...Then he said, "Don't be afraid, Daniel. Since the first day you began to pray for understanding and to humble yourself before your God, your request has been heard in heaven. I have come in answer to your prayer. Daniel 10:2-3,5,12

Daniel fasted for three weeks to receive answers, and the angel of the Lord confirmed that the very *moment* Daniel began praying, things began to move in the supernatural. At the end of the 21 days, God provided those answers and clarity came. This concept may make no sense to our natural minds, but fasting brings supernatural clarity. Fasting exponentiates our prayer intensity and our discernment is heightened as a result. If we want direction for a big decision, healing in a sick body, or favor over an uncertain future, the combination of prayer and fasting is where these blessings begin. Jesus Himself, in Matthew 17:21, said that some miracles could only happen by prayer and fasting. Is there anything weighing on your heart and mind right now that could be relieved by prayer and fasting? What is keeping you from doing so?

God, we want to be empty of the world and full of You. Let us be disciplined at denying our appetites as we remain pure and prepared for Your mission. In Jesus' name we pray this.

36
BALANCE

Balance in our physical health plays a significant role in our spiritual health. The focus of this session is to discuss what the Word says about moderating our pace, exercise, diet, and rest.

Our physical bodies are highly valuable because of their spiritual purpose.

Thank you for making me so wonderfully complex! Your workmanship is marvelous— how well I know it. **Psalm 139:14**

God made each of us intentionally, uniquely, complexly, and marvelously. We are carrying mechanisms of the Holy Spirit. If you were to drive a VIP around in your car tomorrow, who would it be and how would you prepare your car for that person? Why do we treat our bodies any different for Jesus Christ?

There is an indisputable, symbiotic correlation between physical health and spiritual health.

No discipline is enjoyable while it is happening—it's painful! But afterward there will be a peaceful harvest of right living for those...trained in this way. **Hebrews 12:11**

This passage on disciplining a child can be applied on many fronts, one of which is our own physical health. Our flesh is much like a child that needs constraints. And the "peaceful harvest" we all desire in our physical and spiritual health comes at the price of "pain" and inconvenience. Discipline becomes the gateway to getting God's best and being our best. When we fight through discomfort to achieve balance in our physical habits—in our pace of life, exercise, and diet—we simultaneously cultivate restraint that fuels progress in our *spiritual* habits. We realize that the pain we endure by running up the monstrous hill or by saying "no" to the greasy cheeseburger is the same pain we endure by exiting off of the website before falling into sexual temptation or by saying "no" to our comfy pillow at the morning alarm. Remarkable parallels exist between physical and spiritual disciplines. How does *initiating* physical resistance through exercise and fasting help us endure spiritual resistance?

The more conditioned my body is to physical stress, the more prepared my mind is for spiritual stress.

I discipline my body like an athlete, training it to do what it should. Otherwise, I fear that after preaching to others I myself might be disqualified. **1 Corinthians 9:27**

Being in tip-top shape is worthless to God by itself. He doesn't look at our body mass index to determine holiness. However, the mindset that an elite athlete has in making choices based on disciplined principles, not undisciplined feelings, is crucial for the warrior mindset. What area of your physical health could use more balance? Is it a slower pace? More or less food, exercise, or sleep?

Our diet and exercise habits are a part of our worship to God.

...Give your bodies to God because of all He has done for you. Let them be a living and holy sacrifice...This is truly the way to worship Him. **Romans 12:1**

Warriors know we are not on earth to indulge but to invest. And how we care for our physical bodies is an extension of our worship to God. Maintaining balance between the food we consume (in) and energy we expend (out) plays a pivotal role in how we feel. How we feel then greatly impacts the decisions we make. Flesh-led physical health leads to flesh-led spiritual decisions. Spirit-led physical health leads to Spirit-led spiritual decisions. Would you agree that imbalance in our pace, diet, and exercise can compromise our spiritual focus?

We pace and prioritize our schedules to maximize an eternal ROI.

Make the most of every opportunity in these evil days. **Ephesians 5:16**

An unsustainable pace is always the byproduct of a cluttered schedule. We pack our schedules with too many activities, and often with the *wrong* activities. Our busyness becomes burdensome because every engagement is eternally irrelevant. Are the responsibilities in our schedule *allowing* us to sow seeds for eternity or *preventing* us from sowing seeds for eternity elsewhere?

We work hard *and* rest well.

"Fools fold their idle hands, leading them to ruin." And yet, "Better to have one handful with quietness than two handfuls with hard work and chasing the wind." **Ecclesiastes 4:5-6**

Warriors strike a balance between working hard and resting well, and this is not an easy thing to do. Physically and mentally, it is difficult to manage moderation. We don't want to be lazy with folded "idle hands," but we also don't want to overextend obligations, exhausting ourselves by chasing things that don't matter. Would you say you struggle more with laziness or overworking?

True rest, restoration, and refreshment are found only in God's presence.

Those who live in the shelter of the Most High will find rest in the shadow of the Almighty. **Psalm 91:1**

Ample sleep is monumental in maintaining spiritual integrity. Sleep is an essential natural defense for spiritual victory, as it is vital for clarity and sustaining the fruits of the Spirit. However, physical sleep is *not* spiritual rest. Spiritual rest requires time in God's presence, just as this passage reveals. How does worship music play an invaluable role in avoiding burnout and supplying rest to our souls?

We must enjoy a weekly Sabbath to rest and reflect.

You have six days each week for your ordinary work, but the seventh day is a Sabbath day of rest dedicated to the Lord your God... **Exodus 20:9-10**

A day of replenishment and reflection was so important to God that even *He* participated on the seventh day of the universe's existence. No, God didn't *need* rest. He was demonstrating for us how to care for our bodies. What is something you enjoy doing on your weekly Sabbath that refocuses and refreshes you?

God, You gave us physical bodies to accomplish a spiritual purpose. Let us deny our fleshly cravings and live a life of balance and moderation so that we maximize our time here on earth. In Jesus' name we pray this.

37
TRANSPARENCY

Spiritual victory demands transparency with God and with others. The focus of this session is to discuss the necessity of being open and authentic about our sin and growth as warriors.

Transparently confessing our sins to God brings forgiveness and cleansing.

If we claim we have no sin, we are only fooling ourselves and not living in the truth. But if we confess our sins to [God], He is faithful and just to forgive us our sins and to cleanse us from all wickedness. **1 John 1:8-9**

No matter how guilty or dirty we may feel after sins that happened last year or even last night, God is already waiting to forgive us and cleanse us. Why do we instinctively hide in shame and concealment when we mess up? What does *God* desire from us when we have disobeyed Him?

Disobedience brings discipline and guilt; repentance restores peace.

When I refused to confess my sin, my body wasted away, and ...Your hand of discipline was heavy on me. My strength evaporated like water in the summer heat. Finally, I confessed all my sins to You and stopped trying to hide my guilt...And You forgave me! All my guilt is gone. **Psalm 32:3-5**

In this powerful passage written by King David after his affair with Bathsheba, we see that our disobedience often causes our calamity. God allowed a whale to swallow Jonah because he refused to obey and go to Ninevah as instructed. God *will* bring discipline to those who disobey Him, or He will allow the consequences of sin to run their course and wake us up. Have you ever felt the weight lifted, guilt dissolved, and peace restored immediately after confessing sin and doing a 180?

God allows sorrow to draw us to transparency, repentance, and life.

For the kind of sorrow God wants us to experience leads us away from sin and results in salvation. There's no regret for that kind of sorrow. But worldly sorrow, which lacks repentance, results in spiritual death. **2 Corinthians 7:10**

Remorse only says, "I'm sorry," but repentance says, "God, cleanse me with Christ's blood and help me change from the inside out." Sorrow without repentance numbs our spirit man because it lacks Jesus-inspired change in us. We become desensitized to sin. Why is it that we become less appalled by a sin the longer we remain in it?

Transparency makes us aware of our unworthiness.

[Jesus said,] "What sorrow awaits you teachers of religious law and you Pharisees. Hypocrites! For you are like whitewashed tombs—beautiful on the outside but filled on the inside with dead people's bones and all sorts of impurity." **Matthew 23:27**

Pharisees, the religious leaders of Jesus' time, had a legalistic reputation. They knew the laws and were obsessed with obeying them to a T. Their elaborate pious performance served as a facade for corrupt motives and nasty religious pride in their hearts. This cancerous phenomenon sounds like many of us as Christians. We act as if we are "holier than thou," only we have sin embedded in our hearts and habits that are concealed from the world. We may *appear* to be "beautiful" and "whitewashed," but behind the curtain are "all sorts of impurity." At the end of the day, we are all equally unworthy without the blood of Jesus covering us. How does remembering this truth safeguard us from turning a judgmental nose up at those living in sin?

Transparency with other warriors brings healing.

Confess your sins to each other and pray for each other so that you may be healed. The earnest prayer of a righteous person has great power and produces wonderful results. **James 5:16**

Contrary to what sports, military, and business culture reinforce about toughness and masculinity—an unspoken expectation to handle our assignment without assistance or admission of inadequacy—God reveals in this passage that His version of "tough" is vastly different. Toughness is transparency. "Transparent" is the *original* "tough." God's Word tells us that it takes *strength* to admit weakness and vulnerability. And isn't it incredible that when we "man up" and voice our failures and shortcomings, God uses *others* in our healing process. Confession to other warrior brothers prompts supernatural healing, powerful prayer covering, and ultimately, "wonderful results." Since transparency is the path to peace and sin must be exposed before it can be eradicated, why are we so hesitant to reveal what is *really* going on in our lives? Deep down, are we embarrassed to face the reality of sin's prevalence in us?

Transparency about our sexual appetites preserves our purity.

Run from sexual sin! No other sin so clearly affects the body as this one does. For sexual immorality is a sin against your own body. **1 Corinthians 6:18**

Sex is a great gift designed by a great God. But it is far from some casual, recreational activity that should happen between any two people. God intended sex to be a sacred covenant arrangement between one man and one woman in marriage. Because we believe this, we hold sexual intimacy in the highest regard. We are on guard for any influence that cheapens the spiritual significance of sex. We are against sexual intimacy outside of marriage between one man and one woman and *flee* from forces that pique our sexual appetites outside of that context—television, movies, magazines, websites, social media, workplace relationships, dates, business trips, and even public settings. We do whatever it takes to protect our purity by identifying the temptation, taking the thought captive, looking away, saying Jesus' name out loud, voicing a go-to verse from God's Word, praying for power and discipline to endure, and *"running"* away! Why is sexual purity difficult to be transparent about? Could it be because deep down we really don't want to give up the intense pleasure it brings? How does pornography cheapen the sacredness of sex and erode our peace?

Transparency enables purity; purity enhances vision.

God blesses those whose hearts are pure, for they will see God. **Matthew 5:8**

Seeing God has monumental impact, stirring our passion for His calling. Without purity, we lack clear vision, which means impurity brings blindness. What types of impurities can cloud our clarity and compromise our calling as warriors?

God, You know everything about us even when we try to hide sin. Help us embrace transparency as a catalyst for life and peace. We ask that You bind shame, guilt, and regret as we pursue authenticity and purity. In Jesus' name we pray this.

38
ANOINTING

Anointing from God's Spirit fuels us for spiritual victory. The focus of this session is to discuss the Holy Spirit and His role in empowering us for spiritual battle.

Anointing is the result of receiving the Holy Spirit.

[Jesus said,] "But you will receive power when the Holy Spirit comes upon you. And you will be my witnesses, telling people about Me everywhere..." **Acts 1:8**

When we hear the word "anointed," we tend to designate it to religious figures, not ordinary men. However, Acts 2:38 reveals that once we receive Jesus and are baptized in His name, we are anointed. Anointing is simply companionship with the Holy Spirit—the third of the three persons that make up the Trinity (or God's triune being). This particular person—the Holy Spirit—is harder to understand than the other two figures in God's nature (God, the Father and Jesus, the Son) because His role is not as relatable or processable as the roles of father and son. However, the Holy Spirit was Jesus' gift to us as He left earth to go back to heaven. Jesus knew we needed His presence without Him being present, so He gave us His personal Companion—the invisible presence of God—to fill us and help accomplish the mission He gave us. According to this verse in Acts 1, what did Jesus communicate to the first church as the sole purpose of being anointed by the Holy Spirit?

Satan will do everything he can to keep us from receiving the Holy Spirit.

[Jesus said,] "So if you sinful people know how to give good gifts to your children, how much more will your heavenly Father give the Holy Spirit to those who ask Him." **Luke 11:13**

Chris Hodges' book, *Fresh Air*, masterfully unpacks and articulates this beautiful gift of the Holy Spirit and how the enemy *desperately* wants to keep us from experiencing companionship with the Holy Spirit...because the Spirit brings us *victory*. Satan knows that he is destined for defeat in our lives if we embrace and are filled with the Holy Spirit—the very reason the enemy misleads with a misinformation campaign about the Spirit. But despite all the nonsense associations like snake handling or people getting smacked in the head as they fall down on a church stage, the Bible tells us that the Holy Spirit is quiet, powerful, and desirable...not loud, creepy, and repulsive. In fact, the very meaning of the words used in the Greek (Pneuma) *and* Hebrew (Ruach) to describe the Holy Spirit mean "wind" or "breath." Just imagine a scorching hot day when the air is stagnant, stale, and oppressive, and then a refreshing breeze brings us a powerful sigh of relief. *That* is what the Spirit does for our souls, contrary to what misguided religious stereotypes might lead us to believe. God just wants to refresh us and refuel us with this force that cannot be seen but only felt and experienced. Are you in the habit asking God to fill you, refresh you, and direct you with His Holy Spirit? Or have you unknowingly misperceived the Spirit as weird and off-putting?

The Holy Spirit is the perfect Companion.

[Jesus said,] "But when the Father sends the Advocate as my representative—that is, the Holy Spirit—He will teach you everything and will remind you of everything I have told you." **John 14:26**

The Holy Spirit's versatility is unparalleled. Even a Swiss Army knife is laughable compared to the roles that the Spirit plays in helping us. Just look at some of the descriptions of Him throughout Scripture: Wind, Breath, Peace, Power, Strength, Advocate, Helper, Comforter, Teacher, Guide, Friend, Counselor, and Protector. Isaiah 30:21 describes the Spirit as "a voice right behind you" saying, "'This is the way you should go,' whether to the right or to the left." He "teaches" and "reminds" us of everything Jesus lived. What role of the Holy Spirit is most special to you?

Purity is a vacuum for the Holy Spirit's presence.

[Jesus said,] "If you love Me, obey My commandments. And I will ask the Father, and He will give you another Advocate, who will never leave you. He is the Holy Spirit, who leads into all truth. The world cannot receive Him, because it isn't looking for Him and doesn't recognize Him. But you know Him, because He lives with you now and later will be in you." **John 14:15-17**

Jesus is talking to His disciples and makes it clear that He sends His Holy Spirit to fill those who are willing to walk in obedience. So, in order to be filled with the Holy Spirit, I must refuse sin. In response, the Holy Spirit makes me an expert in everything that matters. He "leads [me] into all truth." Is there any impurity in your life that would deter the Holy Spirit from being your supernatural autopilot?

The Holy Spirit is the fuel that empowers my spirit to fight for obedience.

And the Holy Spirit helps us in our weakness. For example, we don't know what God wants us to pray for. But the Holy Spirit prays for us with groanings that cannot be expressed in words. And the Father who knows all hearts knows what the Spirit is saying, for the Spirit pleads for us believers in harmony with God's own will. **Romans 8:26-27**

We do not have the ability to manufacture Jesus' character on our own. Only the Holy Spirit can make us like Jesus. It is our job to simply prevent garbage from occupying the space that the Holy Spirit wants to inhabit. We keep our temples clean to host Him; He uses the space to impress upon others. We acknowledge weakness; He becomes our strength. In what particular area of your life do you especially need the Holy Spirit to "help [you] in [your] weakness"?

The Holy Spirit is a *necessity*, not an option, for spiritual victory.

[Jesus said,] "The Spirit alone gives eternal life. Human effort accomplishes nothing. And the very words I have spoken to you are spirit and life." **John 6:63**

The enemy does not fear us; he fears the Holy Spirit in us. Our charisma, abilities, and efforts do not scare him. We are pathetic and unimpressive without Jesus. What we manufacture on our own is lackluster at best. The artificial fabrication of Jesus that we cast will not attract others to Him. In fact, it is repulsive. The *real* thing—Jesus' character produced by the Holy Spirit—is what draws and inspires people to a relationship with Jesus. The Holy Spirit is who makes others want what we have. He masterfully compensates for our inadequate "human effort" and is a prerequisite of spiritual victory. Why should the Holy Spirit inspire an unshakable confidence in us?

God, Your Holy Spirit gives us hope and freedom. We are honored to receive Your anointing right now and welcome Your Spirit into our lives to empower us for victory. Help us to stay empty to make room for Him. In Jesus' name we pray this.

39
SERVICE

A real relationship with Jesus cultivates service to others. The focus of this session is to discuss what the Word says about serving the people God has placed around us.

Real faith moves us to serve others.

Just as the body is dead without breath, so also faith is dead without good works. **James 2:26**

If we claim to know Jesus Christ and are not actively (and consistently) searching for needs that can be met with our assets, we are lying about our relationship with Jesus. Obedience doesn't save us, but it does demonstrate that we are saved. There is no way we have encountered Jesus if it doesn't spark an uncontainable urgency to bless people and tell them about Him. What are we actually *doing* on a regular basis to serve others?

Service is giving up something of value for someone in need.

We know what real love is because Jesus gave up His life for us. So we also ought to give up our lives for our brothers and sisters. If someone has enough money to live well and sees a brother or sister in need but shows no compassion—how can God's love be in that person? Dear children, let's not merely say that we love each other; let us show the truth by our actions. **1 John 3:16-18**

We serve others by sacrificing something for them. It can be time, talent, food, money, possessions, or even attention. Serving is "show[ing] the truth by our actions." It is fascinating to think that God even programmed our bodies to be rewarded with endorphins by *moving*. We feel better when we move. God rewards movement because life is not about sitting idly and comfortably on the couch. It is about getting up and *doing* something inconvenient...both physically and spiritually. What are some creative ways to show *and* tell people about Jesus?

Leaders serve. Servants lead.

But Jesus called them together and said, "You know that the rulers in this world lord it over their people, and officials flaunt their authority over those under them. But among you it will be different. Whoever wants to be a leader among you must be your servant, and whoever wants to be first among you must become your slave. For even the Son of Man came not to be served but to serve others and to give His life as a ransom for many." **Matthew 20:25-28**

Jesus is the model of masculine leadership—a King who serves. Does it make us strong or weak as men to lift up and serve those under our authority?

When we serve a person, we serve Jesus.

[Jesus said,] "I tell you the truth, when you [served] one of the least of these my brothers and sisters, you were [serving] Me!" **Matthew 25:40**

Service ignores status and significance. It is effortless to serve someone who has much to offer in return, but forfeiting something for a person who cannot repay you whatsoever—"the least of these"—is what touches the heart of God. And isn't it wild that Jesus said we are literally serving Him when we serve them? Have we trained ourselves to see *Jesus'* eyes when we look into the eyes of others?

The proof is in the serving.

If you are wise and understand God's ways, prove it by living an honorable life, doing good works with the humility that comes from wisdom. **James 3:13**

When we understand God's nature, we recognize that we are *all* called to full-time ministry, just in different locations. You might be advancing the Kingdom in a factory while another man is doing so in a fire station. Location is irrelevant. Ministry is eminent. We do not need more ministers *visiting* the factories and fire stations; we need more factory workers and fire fighters to *be* ministers. The proof that we love Jesus is in the "honorable life" and "good works" that we bring into our workplaces and communities. Has God ever inspired a dream or an idea of how you can utilize your passions to bless your sphere of influence?

Warriors are servant fighters.

The laborers carried on their work [building the wall] with one hand supporting their load and one hand holding a weapon... **Nehemiah 4:17**

Nehemiah was a man with a practical mind and strong faith. He knew how to get things done, like rebuilding the wall around Jerusalem in just 52 days. During that 52-day period, enemies threatened to "swoop down and kill them and end their work," but Nehemiah strategically led the Jews to work and battle simultaneously. As we serve, we must fight against the enemy's schemes to exploit vulnerabilities and "end our work." And we must be prepared to do the two in tandem—serve *and* fight. We build with one hand and protect with the other. Who can testify to the satisfaction of serving and the fulfillment of fighting?

God gifted you to serve others.

God has given each of you a gift from His great variety of spiritual gifts. Use them well to serve one another. Do you have the gift of speaking? Then speak as though God Himself were speaking through you. Do you have the gift of helping others? Do it with all the strength and energy that God supplies. Then everything you do will bring glory to God through Jesus Christ... **1 Peter 4:10-11**

In our children's journey to "discover" their identity on earth, we as fathers should tell them to be as unique as they want to be...to be different...to be dynamic...to "be you"...but with one *major* stipulation—to "be you" *within* the confines of God's Word. The moment we step outside the boundaries God instituted is the moment we step over to the Tree of the Knowledge of Good and Evil—where it becomes about us. Our unique stories and giftings are our most valuable possessions...*if* we use them to point to the blood of the Lamb. There are almost two dozen "spiritual gifts" listed in Romans 12, Ephesians, 4, and 1 Corinthians 12-13, including teaching, leadership, giving, and servanthood. What gifts and attributes do you believe God gave you to dynamically serve His church?

God, You created us not to sit still but to move as we *show* others who Jesus is. No matter our position, humble us to be servants just like Your Son and to pinpoint opportunities to be a blessing to others. In Jesus' name we pray this.

40
LEGACY

Warriors live to leave a legacy for Jesus. The focus of this session is to discuss how to be intentional about leaving an impression that lasts forever.

We steadfastly live every moment for our final moment on earth.

And what do you benefit if you gain the whole world but lose your own soul? Is anything worth more than your soul? **Matthew 26:16**

Every road we travel that doesn't lead to Jesus is a dead end. We may conquer everything under the sun and make billions of dollars in the process, but all of it will mean nothing if the enemy conquers our souls in the process. Legacy is a life lived in a shadow, not a spotlight. As Galatians 6:14 says, "As for me, may I never boast about anything except the cross of our Lord Jesus Christ." This cements an impact that endures beyond the earth. We as warriors are bold, and as 2 Corinthians 6:8 says, "We serve God whether people honor us or despise us, whether they slander us or praise us." We do not care about what people think about us. If we died today, could we confidently say we lived in a way that made our last moment our best moment?

Legacy is about living like Jesus, not just knowing about Jesus.

If someone claims, "I know God," but doesn't obey God's commandments, that person is a liar and is not living in the truth. But those who obey God's word truly show how completely they love Him. That is how we know we are living in Him. Those who say they live in God should live their lives as Jesus did. **1 John 2:4-6**

Our legacy is not about how much theological doctrine we know, but about how much of Jesus' life we show. Warriors "show how completely [we] love [God]" by "living [our] lives as Jesus did." A man becomes dynamic in today's culture simply living for Jesus. Wherever we go, we cultivate God's presence. In our cars, homes, or offices, we shut down secular influences like music and movies that seductively and romantically package up lies, replacing them with worshipful messaging that aligns with God's Word. Why is it important for our families to hear us say, "I was wrong, I am sorry, and please forgive me" when we fail to "live [our] lives as Jesus did"?

We steward our children as our most cherished legacy.

Children are a gift from the Lord; they are a reward from Him. Children born to a young man are like arrows in a warrior's hands. **Psalm 127:3-4**

Our most enduring legacy will be reflected by the people inside our homes. How we steward our influence in our households will outlast every other impression we leave behind. Our children are watching. They are listening, too. But they will stop listening if what they *hear* from us doesn't match what they *see* from us. Our lifestyles trump our lectures. What are some specific ways we can shape our children—these impressionable "arrows" in our hands—to be like Jesus? Why is attending and serving the local church week in and week out crucial to establishing a worthwhile legacy?

We intentionally engage with our children and teach them God's Word.

"Direct your children onto the right path, and when they are older, they will not leave it." **Proverbs 22:6**

God promises that when we point our children to the Word again and again, "they will not leave it." This doesn't mean they won't sin or stray for a season, but it does mean that once they've tasted the filet mignon that is God's Word, they'll never be satisfied by the dog food that is the world. We must solidify our children's footing in God's Word by engaging with them. We don't just engage them; we engage *with* them. There's a big difference. We don't allow technology to raise our kids, nor do we allow technology to distract *us* from raising our children. Apps, video games, and TV entertainment are horrible parents, which is why we must be present and intentionally engage with our kids so that one day we can voice 3 John 1:4: "I could have no greater joy than to hear that my children are following the truth." Is it possible for us to raise our kids, lead our wives, run our businesses, manage our money, and live our lives based on a book if *we* don't know the book?

Legacy comes from leaving it all on the battlefield for our kids...every day.

My child, don't reject the Lord's discipline, and don't be upset when He corrects you. For the Lord corrects those He loves, just as a father corrects a child in whom he delights. **Proverbs 3:11-12**

Raising disciplined children can be exhausting at times, especially when we are trying to strike a balance between grace and truth, but our children crave God's boundaries whether they realize it or not. Lazily avoiding confrontation may gain our children's popularity, but it will come at the expense of their respect. As fathers, would you rather have *popularity with* your children now or *respect from* your children later? As sons (of every age), how do we honor the love behind our parents' advice and discipline even when we don't like it or agree with it? How important is our *attitude* when we obey our parents?

We invest time, energy, and resources into spreading the Gospel.

The rain and snow come down from the heavens and stay on the ground to water the earth. They cause the grain to grow, producing seed for the farmer and bread for the hungry. It is the same with My word. I send it out, and it always produces fruit. It will accomplish all I want it to, and it will prosper everywhere I send it. **Isaiah 55:10-11**

When we consume and share the Word, it will always yield fruit, even when we do not see it. We must focus on our responsibility and let God handle the results. If just a remnant emerges years down the road from our hard work, it will all be worth it. Famed financial investor Warren Buffett once said, "The stock market is a device for transferring money from the impatient to the patient." Investments are about patience. We don't *spend* our time and resources; we *invest* them. Spending attains something instantly that depreciates over time. Investing sacrifices something now that appreciates over time. Kingdom investments may require patience, but they pay off in the future. How are we personally "sending out" God's Word in our lives so that it can "accomplish" and "prosper" what God desires?

God, nothing we accomplish on earth matters except the people we lead to Your Son, Jesus. Let our lives be lived for the moment we meet You, and let our legacy be cemented for eternity as a result. In Jesus' name we pray this.

41
UNITY

Unity enables exponential impact in spiritual war. The focus of this session is to discuss how unity in and for Jesus is an unstoppable catalyst for victory.

God made us to be united under His authority.

Make every effort to keep yourselves united in the Spirit, binding yourselves together with peace. For there is one body and one Spirit, just as you have been called to one glorious hope for the future. There is one Lord, one faith, one baptism, one God and Father of all, who is over all, in all, and living through all. **Ephesians 4:3-6**

Life is all about God. Every human being in the universe was made by one God for one purpose—to know Him and make Him known. Any departure from this theology is human-contrived and based on a lie. Every man-made theory or cause either unites us for a secondary purpose or separates us from our primary purpose. What are some purposes (both good and bad) for which people unite?

Satan uses pride to divide and create sides.

I appeal to you, dear brothers and sisters, by the authority of our Lord Jesus Christ, to live in harmony with each other. Let there be no divisions in the church. Rather, be of one mind, united in thought and purpose. **1 Corinthians 1:10**

Whenever there is division, we quickly pinpoint *people* who are to blame, but reality is, the people are never the problem. Ephesians 6:12 tells us that behind every person that appears to be the problem is a spiritual enemy who *is* the problem. The devil divides. He may use people as his medium of choice to wage war, but people are not our enemy. Satan is. Like a puppeteer pulling the strings, his goal is to manipulate us into running his play, not God's. So as the metaphor goes, "Don't shoot the messenger," because the real problem is not the person but the enemy's work within that person. Oswald Chambers said this in his book, *My Utmost for His Highest*, about our response to sin and division: "When we discern that other people are not growing spiritually and allow that discernment to turn to criticism, we block our fellowship with God. God never gives us discernment so that we may criticize, but that we may intercede." When we see others departed from God's way, do we point our fingers at them or fight against the enemy in prayer for them?

Unity leverages individual talents for compounding victory.

Just as our bodies have many parts and each part has a special function, so it is with Christ's body. We are many parts of one body, and we all belong to each other. In His grace, God has given us different gifts for doing certain things well. **Romans 12:4-6**

The inner core of every man craves to collaborate with other men for a purpose greater than himself. We all long to be a part of something big—something high-stakes that actually *matters*—and we aspire to be associated with other men doing larger-than-life things. It is why are drawn to exceptional teamwork that innovates, revolutionizes, and dominates its space like the U.S. military, Tesla, Apple, or the Alabama football dynasty in the 2000's. We hunger for significance that is only created by *unity*. We magnetize toward collaborative excellence because it makes us feel alive. But no collaboration—no unity—makes us feel more alive and significant than when we unite with other men for spiritual battle. Engaging in the mission to tell others about Jesus—strategizing with our brothers to plan and resource this preeminent initiative—quenches all the longings of a man. But we must *participate* to experience it. Unity requires participation. What "special function" do you believe God intended you to "do well" alongside other warriors in spiritual battle?

Unity demands humility.

Live in harmony with each other. Don't be too proud to enjoy the company of ordinary people. And don't think you know it all! **Romans 12:16**

Pride and unity are like water and oil. They do not mix well. A man who thinks too highly of himself will see others through the clouded lens of superiority. The enemy delights in this phenomenon. He wants us to be endlessly irritated by the differences of others and turn us against one another. He will use anything he can—skin color, ethnicity, gender, physical fitness, education, political preference, account balance, social status, spiritual beliefs—to drive a wedge of animosity between us. But Jesus doesn't take sides. He was humbly crucified in the *middle* of two criminals. His way is *the* way, not the left or the right. Humility moves us to the middle to focus on what we have *in common*—the image of God—so we can love others as Christ did. How do both favoritism and discrimination devalue the image of God in certain people?

Unity in Jesus is *always* the answer to the division and discord sin creates.

[Jesus said,] "For where two or three gather together as my followers, I am there among them." **Matthew 18:20**

Whenever we abandon God's principles, we open the door for division and destruction. Spiritual depravity gives the devil unhindered access to create chaos— the very reason we as warriors despise sin and avoid it at all costs. Where God isn't present, sin can abound. And where sin abounds, it is free to pervert itself exponentially and mutate into more disturbing strains. Morality alone is no match for the progression of sin; only God's presence protects and heals us from the comprehensive decay of sin. If Jesus is literally present in rooms with two or more disciples gathered in His name, won't more healing and unity take place the more frequently we meet?

Our health and strength are dependent upon physically meeting together.

Let us think of ways to motivate one another to acts of love and good works. And let us not neglect our meeting together, as some people do, but encourage one another, especially now that the day of His return is drawing near. **Hebrews 10:24-25**

Virtual (online) relationships cannot replace real ones. The spiritual fire that ignites when God's people come together *physically* in a space to worship Him is unparalleled. Not to mention, in-person social interaction has been scientifically proven to improve our mental, emotional, and physical health. This truth was only magnified during 2020 when the worldwide COVID-19 pandemic forced us all into isolation. Why is social media a terrible replacement for real-life relationships? And how can virtual interactions divide us and make it difficult to "work at living in peace with everyone," as Hebrews 12:14 encourages us to do?

God, no organization or legislation can bring perfect peace and unity. Only Jesus can. Let us as warriors remain unified in Him and focused on spiritual victory. In Jesus' name we pray this.

42
JESUS

Jesus is the quintessential Warrior. The focus of this session is to discuss the real, raw, expansive power and deep, authentic, intimate love that gives us spiritual victory as warriors for Him.

Every man is just a man. Except Jesus.

You were dead because of your sins and because your sinful nature was not yet cut away. Then God made you alive with Christ, for He forgave all our sins. He canceled the record of the charges against us and took it away by nailing it to the cross. In this way, He disarmed the spiritual rulers and authorities. He shamed them publicly by His victory over them on the cross. **Colossians 2:13-15**

Reflecting on Jesus' insane victory will give us remarkable passion. But make no mistake about it...we must reflect regularly on Jesus' "disarm[ing]" darkness in order to remain excited about the Gospel. Our passion for Jesus hinges on our inserting Him into the *now*, even placing Him side-by-side with the iconic figures in society to realize that there *is* no comparison. Jesus stands alone as an incomparable superpower. Nothing any mortal man has done or will do is even remotely impressive when put beside the sole super-heroic one-two combo of the baffling, blood-saturated cross and chilling, air-infested tomb of the Man, Jesus Christ. It helps to place Jesus smack dab next to the "impressive" things that *are* visible and *can* be comprehended on earth—gifted people, heroic feats, or forces of nature—so that we can at least scratch the surface of comprehending just how much more mind-blowing Jesus' death-defeating power is. We will never fully comprehend it, but trying to do so is what keeps us fired up to fight in victory. Who or what impresses you most on this earth?

Jesus loves sinners but despises sin.

Jesus entered the Temple and began to drive out all the people buying and selling animals for sacrifice. He knocked over the tables of the money changers and the chairs of those selling doves. He said to them, "The Scriptures declare, 'My Temple will be called a house of prayer,' but you have turned it into a den of thieves!" **Matthew 21:12-13**

Jesus aggressively addressed the sin in His temple in this passage. First Corinthians 6:19 tells us *we* are His temple. Therefore, once we know Jesus, He wants us to aggressively confront sin in our lives. Jesus is gentle toward people, but not toward sin in people. What sin has God driven out of your temple?

Seeing Jesus daily in worship equips us with passion for spiritual victory.

When I saw [the Son of Man], I fell at His feet as if I were dead. But [Jesus] laid His right hand on me and said, "Don't be afraid! I am the First and the Last. I am the living one. I died, but look—I am alive forever and ever! And I hold the keys of death and the grave." **Revelation 1:17-18**

John reveals to us in this passage the ultimate weapon of spiritual victory—an *encounter* with Jesus. It goes beyond knowledge of Jesus; it is knowing Him by being in close proximity. By *seeing* Jesus one time, we are changed. The greatest discipline of Christian manhood is to deliberately immerse ourselves in the *reality* of the crucifixion and resurrection of Christ on a daily basis. To turn on worship music and actually transport ourselves—physically, mentally, and spiritually—to the foot of the bloody cross and empty tomb of Jesus. If we do this, we will win every battle in decisive fashion because it equips us with both His *love*—that gentle passion for us on the cross—and His *power*—that unmatchable force in the resurrection. How often do we turn on worship music, close our eyes, and go to these momentous moments in or minds? How do meditation on Jesus' love and power and identification with Jesus' death and resurrection motivate us to fight for obedience?

Jesus is fully God, fully Man, and fully victorious.

For in Christ lives all the fullness of God in a human body. So you also are complete through your union with Christ, who is the head over every ruler and authority. **Colossians 2:9-10**

It may be difficult for us to understand, but God manifested Himself completely as a Man through Jesus Christ. While Jesus is fully Man, He is also fully God. Jesus' humanity made Him capable of feeling every temptation and emotion we face as humans, but His unbroken unity with the Holy Spirit is what made Jesus incapable of sinning. This is a tremendous lesson for us as men: We too can be "perfect" like God (Matthew 5:48) if we are covered by Jesus' blood and moment-by-moment remain connected to the Holy Spirit. What keeps us from unbroken unity with God's Spirit?

Jesus is the worthy, victorious Lion.

... "Stop weeping! Look, the Lion of the tribe of Judah, the heir to David's throne, has won the victory. He is worthy to open the scroll and its seven seals." **Revelation 5:5**

We wake up every day focused on *our* lives. We live inside a script that makes *us* the protagonist—the main character in our tale. But this is so far from reality. *Jesus* is the story. Men are mere footnotes. All of us. The universe's entire infrastructure revolves around the spotless Lamb who was slain (John 1:29) and the unrivaled Lion who defeated death and ascended into heaven. In Him, we have *roaring* victory. Have you ever roared for a sports victory or a personal accomplishment? It may be a peculiar question to some, but have you ever roared for Jesus' resurrection victory?

Jesus is coming back to earth.

Look! [Jesus] comes with the clouds of heaven. And everyone will see Him—even those who pierced Him. And all the nations of the world will mourn for Him. Yes! Amen! "I am the Alpha and the Omega—the beginning and the end," says the Lord God. "I am the one who is, who always was, and who is still to come—the Almighty One." **Revelation 1:7-8**

There will be theories galore on mainstream media outlets trying to make sense out of how so many humans inexplicably disappeared when God raptures "the remnant" that is His church (Romans 9:27). But think about the Second Coming of Jesus—His return to establish His Kingdom on earth. At the "blast of a trumpet" people "will see the Son of Man coming on the clouds of heaven with power and great glory" (Matthew 24:30-31). Imagine the videos from every angle that will be posted of Jesus' radiant return to earth into Jerusalem. It will defy logic. It is reason to put our faith in Jesus and tell as many people as possible before it is too late. The moment "will come as unexpectedly as a thief," as Revelation 16:15 says. What part of Jesus' return pumps you up most? Who around you needs to know Jesus before His return happens?

God, we are victorious warriors like Your Son. Let us be united as real men who fight in the victory of Jesus for the things of Jesus. In Jesus' name we pray this. Amen.

Acknowledgments

To my *treasure* of a wife—Brooke Gilleo Ingram—thank you for supporting me and for encouraging me throughout this three-year project. You are an unbelievable woman of God, spouse, and mother. You are my greatest blessing, and I thank God every day that He granted me a bombshell woman of such strength and humility. I love you so much.

To my children—Crew, Oakland, and Natalee—your Daddy and Mommy love you five-finity, maybe even ten-finity. As your Jana says, always...always...shine for Jesus.

To my parents—Burr and Jan Ingram—you two are as dynamic as they come. Between your solid consistency, Dad, and your joyful selflessness, Mom, I've never known a couple more distinct than you two. Thank you for raising your boys to live for Jesus and for modeling what that looks like.

To my brothers—Rob and Mack Ingram—I am so grateful for the relationship we have and for the men of God you are. You sharpen me.

To my friend and mentor—Rick Burgess—your fixation on God's mission has inspired me to be a more focused disciple of Jesus. Thank you for believing in me and with me from the first day I mentioned this dynamic project.

To my legendary pastor—Chris Hodges—I have absorbed your Spirit-filled teaching and leadership at Church of the Highlands for the last 13 years, and your imprint in this resource is undeniable. I am walking in my calling because of your obedience.

To my fellow warrior and content editor—Adam Tyson—you are a standout pastor, teacher, and disciple of Jesus. Thank you for lending your theological expertise and Spirit-filled wisdom to this project.

To my grammatical editor—Kristie Garner—you are a fantastic editor. Thank you for making sense of my writing and for making this project excellent.

To my close circle of warrior men—you all know who you are—thank you for pushing me to finish this God-given assignment and for praying this entire project into existence.

To each man who reads this Bible study—*fight* to be the warrior God made you to be, and take to heart this challenging reminder from Greek philosopher, Heraclitus, of how rare a true warrior is:

"Out of every hundred men, ten shouldn't be there, eighty are just targets, nine are the real fighters, and we are lucky to have them, for they make the battle. Ah, but the one, one is a warrior, and he will bring the others back."

Lance Ingram, Author of *United For Victory* Group Guide